CONVERSATIONS OF THE

SAINTS

CONVERSATIONS OF THE

SAINTS

Words of Wisdom From God's Chosen

BERNARD-MARIE, O.F.S., AND JEAN HUSCENOT, F.É.C.

TRANSLATED BY VICTORIA HÉBERT AND DENIS SABOURIN

Liguori
LIGUORI, MISSOURI

Published by Liguori Publications
Liguori, Missouri
http://www.liguori.org

Library of Congress Cataloging-in-Publication Data

Bernard-Marie, Brother, O.F.S.
    [Paroles de saints, English]
Conversations of the saints : words of wisdom from God's chosen /
Bernard-Marie, O.F.S., Jean Huscenot, translated by Victoria Hébert and
Denis Sabourin. 1st. U.S. ed.
     p. cm.
    Includes index.
    ISBN 0-7648-0386-7
    1. Spiritual life—Catholic Church—Quotations, maxims, etc. 2.
Christian saints—Quotations. I. Huscenot, Jean. II. Title.
BX2350.2.B4276   1999
282'.062'2—dc21
[B]   98–37432

First published in France as *Paroles de Saints leurs réparties les plus
percutantes* by Éditions Brepols, Paris, 1995.

Printed in the United States of America
First U.S. Edition
03 02 01   6 5 4 3

TABLE OF CONTENTS

INTRODUCTION

When baptized believers look for additional enlightenment for their Christian faith, they usually turn to the Gospels, the sacraments, prayer, and often also toward the Fathers of the Church and the recent magisterial documents. As well, they look to a variety of theological and spiritual writings that originate from different thinkers and witnesses and unite a certain number of ecclesiastical guarantees. They are certainly correct to act in this manner because it was truly the Holy Spirit who inspired the apostles and then all the leaders and Doctors of the Church who are worthy of these titles.

All the same, another source of spirituality also exists which is not frequently consulted. In this book, we address the concrete lives of the saints—more precisely, their spontaneous conversations with their contemporaries. These exchanges are often surprisingly profound. The history of the Church shows that the saints could give the best of themselves when their surroundings placed them in a situation of having to defend the interests of God, or as Peter says, "Always be ready to make your defense to anyone who demands from you an accounting for the hope that is in you; yet do it with gentleness and reverence" (1 Pet 3:15–16).

Should we be surprised to find that the Holy Spirit then granted his gentle and penetrating assistance to the saints in the form of spontaneous conversations, generally not formally written down? If so, this surprise would belie the fact that the Holy Spirit does not work for posterity but for eternity, and that salvation is not for the future but for right now—only, however, if humans freely agree to it.

Another reason exists why the Holy Spirit intervenes so faithfully in the daily lives of truly evangelical persons. He does this to carry out Christ's solemn promise which we too often have a tendency to forget or to water down. Jesus had, in effect, promised his disciples that when they would be brought before the tribunals or were required to justify their faith before others, they would not be preoccupied with what they would have to say. "For what you are to say will be given to you at that time; for it is not you who speak, but the Spirit of your Father speaking through you" (Mt 10:19–20). From this we can conclude that there exists a testament of the inspired words of the saints. This would even include the words of future saints—some of whom are easy to spot among us, although in these cases, discernment is more difficult given that we do not enjoy the benefit of hindsight.

The challenge we have undertaken in the pages of this book is to look into the lives of the saints and collect their most beautiful and inspiring statements—those which are truly authentic messages of the light of the Holy Spirit, in order to provide spiritual support for the reader. This type of compendium without a doubt could lead to others. We could, for example, imagine a compendium of the divine comments of the Most High, gathered from the Bible. There, we would certainly find answers such as this one from the Almighty to Job: "Where were you when I laid the foundation of the earth? Tell me, if you have understanding" (Job 38:4). Or Jesus' famous reply to the Pharisees: "Give therefore to the emperor the things that are the emperor's, and to God the things that are God's" (Mt 22:21).

Because he was a prophet, and so much more than just a prophet, Jesus could, with assurance, discern with his friends what came from above, from below, or simply from the hearts of human beings. This is also the reason he could allow himself to say to Peter: "Blessed are you, Simon son of Jonah! For flesh and blood has not revealed this to you, but my Father in heaven" (Mt 16:17). With confidence and humility, we have worked to walk in the footsteps of our Lord and have endeavored to locate, in the lives of the saints those proclaimed words which are given under the guidance, influence, and genuine movement of the Holy Spirit.

Here then, is a testament of the Holy Spirit which owes nothing to a sudden cathartic illumination. Now, in our turn, let us find and follow these enlightening words of the saints and make them our own spiritual food! It would be a great joy if our own words could, at times, be fertilized by the Holy Spirit who would, then, speak in us and with us for the salvation of many. Deep inside ourselves, however, we already know what brings on the favors of the Holy Spirit and transforms the humblest of believers into a true prophet of our heavenly Father—it is the act of withstanding trials and persecutions in the name of Christ with the utmost patience and love. In this sense, the most precious of all Christ's words when he hung on the cross was his accepting smile when faced with the will of God, his loving gaze toward his neighbor, and the gift of his prayerful silence. Let us remember this silent and accepting acquiescence even as we come to the last page of this collection of words of the saints.

BERNARD-MARIE, O.F.S.
JEAN HUSCENOT, F.É.C.

REFERENCE NOTES TO THE READER

- Bible references are from *The New Revised Standard Version* (Catholic Edition), 1989.
- The words reported here are generally short and meaningful and are taken from the best lives of the saints available. Sources for the works used are cited after each quotation. In this way, a reader interested in pursuing any material further may find the necessary volume(s) to do so. Subsequent references to the same source are given in shortened form.
- The initial biographical details as well as the notes conveying historical context that surround each citation are the work of the authors.
- Certain gaps in the chronological progression of the centuries (for example, the sixth to the eleventh centuries) are a result of a dearth of reliable historical material available for these time periods. Especially lacking are the particular type of spontaneous conversations that are the subject of this book.
- A few citations belong to the traditional recountings of the foundations of a religious order or diocese. These kinds of citations are difficult to source precisely, but given a high degree of interest in them and their consistency with what is known about a saint, we believe it is appropriate to include them anyway—at least until better sources are available.
- It goes without saying that, for us, this subject is not closed. We would welcome all serious suggestions for additional information or corrections that could be applied to this

work. In spite of the occasional use of references to sources that are attributed to accepted traditions, our objective has always been to create an authentic history and not just a collection of anecdotes for easy edification. It is that concern that moved us to limit the length of this work.

SAINT PETER
LEADER OF THE APOSTLES

orn in Bethsaida, but established as a fisherman on Lake Tiberias (Sea of Galilee) in the village of Capernaum, Simon, the brother of Andrew, would be named Peter by Jesus. Whether or not Peter died in 64 A.D. at the time of Nero's persecution, the Gospels sketch a contrasting portrait of him. Here we present a few examples, marked by the seal of the Holy Spirit.

A STRONG FAITH

[Jesus] said to them, "But who do you say that I am?"

Simon Peter answered, "You are the Messiah, the Son of the living God."

Mt 16:15–16.

A TRUE FAITHFULNESS

So Jesus asked the twelve, "Do you wish to go away?"

Simon Peter answered him, "Lord, to whom can we go? You have the words of eternal life."

Jn 6:67–68.

A COURAGEOUS SPONTANEITY

Jesus said to [Peter], "Truly I tell you, this day, this very night, before the cock crows twice, you will deny me three times."

But [Peter] said vehemently, "Even though I must die with you, I will not deny you."

Mk 14:30–31.

A FRIENDSHIP WITHOUT QUESTION

[Jesus said] to him…, "Simon son of John, do you love me?"

And [Peter] said to him, "Lord, you know everything; you know that I love you."

Jn 21:17.

Saint Thomas

APOSTLE

Nicknamed "Didymus" (the twin), Thomas appears many times in the Gospel of John. Was he a disbelieving skeptic in principle? In any event, it seems that he was gifted with a real sense of generosity. We will meditate on two of his superb exclamations, which reveal a man who was totally devoted.

DISCIPLE UNTIL DEATH

[Jesus] said to the disciples, "Let us go to Judea again." (After having heard that Lazarus was seriously ill.)

The disciples said to him, "Rabbi, the Jews were just now trying to stone you, and are you going there again?"

[Jesus] told them, "Our friend Lazarus has fallen asleep, but I am going there to awaken him."

Thomas said to his fellow disciples: "Let us also go, that we may die with him (Jesus)."

Jn 11:7–16.

ULTIMATE PROFESSION OF FAITH

[The arisen Jesus] said to Thomas, "Put your finger here and see my hands. Reach out your hand and put it in my side. Do not doubt but believe."

Thomas answered him, "My Lord and my God!"

Jn 20:27–29.

Saint Ignatius of Antioch

BISHOP

I gnatius (in Greek: the Burning), nicknamed Theophore (the messenger of God), died a martyr in 107 A.D. He was Bishop of Antioch, Syria, for forty years.

The Supreme Testimony

Under Emperor Trajan, Bishop Ignatius was arrested and transferred in stages to Rome, to be thrown to the beasts. During the trip, he met various leaders of the Christian communities. They told him of their desire to intervene on his behalf so that his sentence would be commuted, perhaps even canceled.

Ignatius responded with the following words, which he also wrote for them, "It is with a good heart that I am going to die for God, that is, if you don't stop me. I beg you, do not have an inopportune concern for me! Let me become fodder for the beasts, because through them, it will be possible for me to find God. I am the wheat of God. I want to be milled by the teeth of the beasts and through this, I will become a pure bread of Christ. My childbirth approaches. Brothers, forgive me and do not stop my progression to Life. Those who wish to belong to God are not of this world!...

My taste for earthly things has been crucified, there is no more fire in me to love things, but only a living water which whispers in me: 'Come to the Father!'..."

"Letter to the Romans," IV–VII, from The Writings of the Apostolic Fathers, trans. Camelot, Cerf: Paris, 1963, pp. 172–175.

SAINT POLYCARP
BISHOP

Notable witness to the faith of the second century, Bishop of Smyrna, Saint Polycarp was a disciple of the apostle John and teacher of the young Irenaeus of Lyon. He died a martyr around 155 A.D.

A BEAUTIFUL EXAMPLE OF FAITHFULNESS

The Roman Proconsul, Statius Quadratus, sought to make Polycarp renounce Christ, saying, "Swear allegiance to Caesar, damn Christ, and I will let you go."

Polycarp replied, "I have been serving Him for eighty-six years and He has never wronged me. How then could I renounce this King who has saved me?"

"Martyrdom of Polycarp" in The Writings of the Apostolic Fathers, trans., Camelot, Cerf: Paris, 1963, p. 227.

PROFESSION AT THE PRICE OF BLOODSHED

The Proconsul said again to Polycarp, "I have beasts and I will deliver you to them if you don't change your mind."

Polycarp replied, "Then call them, because it is impossible for me to change my mind. If I did, it would be like going from better to worse."

Again the Proconsul said, "Then I will burn you at the stake since you put my beasts down.

Polycarp responded, "This fire will burn for only a moment and go out. There is another fire that lasts forever, the one that is reserved for the ungodly. Don't hesitate. Go ahead, do what you wish!"

"Martyrdom of Polycarp," p. 228.

SAINT JUSTIN
PHILOSOPHER

Justin was born of Greek parents, around 100 A.D., at Naplouse, in Palestine. He studied philosophy under various Greek teachers and, when he was about thirty years old, he was converted to Christianity after being impressed by the martyrs and after being introduced to the Old Testament prophets. The following writings are credited to him: *An Apology of the Christian Religion* and *Dialogues with the Jew Tryphon*. He died in 165, decapitated along with other Christians, in Rome.

THE ROMAN GODS OR CHRIST

In Rome, at the tribunal, the prefect, Rusticus, questioned Justin, asking, "Why don't you submit to the gods and obey the emperors?... If you are whipped, then decapitated, do you believe that afterwards you will rise to heaven?"

Justin answered, "If I endure all of that, I hope to find my home there! I also know that divine reward is reserved for those who would endure these things."

Rusticus replied, "You think then, that you will rise to heaven to receive rewards?"

Justin then said, "I don't think it, I am convinced of it!"

To which Rusticus replied, "You and your friends, come closer and sacrifice yourselves to the gods!"

Triumphantly, Justin answered, "No man, unless he has lost his mind, would abandon the Truth, once he has found it!"

Justin Martyr: Complete Works, "Acts of the Martyr,"
trans. Hamman & B.M., Migne-Brepols: Paris, 1994, pp. 365–368.

Saint Monica
Mother

M onica (332–387) was a native of Carthage. She married a pagan and had three children, among them the
future Saint Augustine, Doctor of the Church. In her
goodness, she brought her husband to the Christian faith.
She accompanied Augustine to Italy and, by her prayers, she
obtained his conversion in 386, a year before she died.

An Indestructible Hope

After living for some time in Ostia with Augustine,
Monica envisaged returning to North Africa, but delayed in
getting the project underway. A friend of her son, knowing
of the plan, asked one day, "By living here, do you not fear
the possibility (if you die), of having your body buried so far
from home?"

Answering him, Monica replied, "Nothing is too far away
for God! At the end of time, He will know where to find my
body to resurrect it."

Confessions, Saint Augustine, Book IX, Ch. 11, trans. J. Trabucco,
Garnier-Flammarion: Paris, 1964, p. 196.

A Solid Hierarchy of Values

At the age of sixty-four and still living in Ostia, Monica
caught a fever and suffered a type of weakness that caused
her to lose consciousness. Coming to, she saw her two sons
next to her. She firmly stated to them, "You will bury your
mother here!"

Augustine's brother then said, "How lucky you would be if you could die at home and not here in a foreign land."

Monica then replied, "See what your brother (Augustine) would suggest, but you two, don't do anything special to my body. Bury it wherever you wish. I only ask that you remember me before the Altar of God, wherever you may be."

Confessions, Book IX, Ch. 11, p. 195–6.

Saint Ambrose of Milan
Bishop

A high Roman magistrate, Ambrose was designated Bishop of Milan in 374 by popular acclamation. This consul of God (339–397) contributed to the conversion of Saint Augustine. Monica, the mother of the latter, had prepared the way for this.

A Consoling Prophecy

Monica did not hesitate to go to Milan to secure the assistance of Ambrose, a spiritual leader who was said to be capable of responding to all heretical arguments. Monica said to Ambrose, "My son (Augustine) has embarrassed more than one simple spirit by his objections."

Ambrose replied, "Leave him be! All you have to do is pray for him. One day, his readings will make him recognize his errors and impieties on his own."

Monica pleaded, "I beg you: please meet with him and agree to discuss this."

But Ambrose said, "Go in peace. As true as you are now standing before me, the son of such tears will not know death!"

"And my mother," adds Augustine, "received these words as if they had been said to her from heaven."

Confessions, Saint Augustine, Book III, Ch. 12, p. 64.

SAINT DANIEL THE STYLITE
PRIEST AND MONK

D aniel (409–493) was a monk in a convent in Syro-Palestine. Impressed by the example of Saint Simeon the Stylite, who lived near Antioch, he decided to follow his example and dedicate the last thirty-three years of his life to living atop a pillar, near Constantinople.

ONLY LOVE IS NECESSARY FOR SALVATION

A rich man questioned Daniel, then eighty years old, "As you have been up on that pillar for the past thirty years, what advice can you give me, noble champion?

Daniel answered, "Love your neighbor, especially the poor. Up until today, you have loved no one but yourself. In truth, very little!"

"Apophtegmes" in Patrologia Latina, J. P. Migne, t. 80, col. 137ff.

Saints John and Barsanuphius of Gaza
Desert Hermits

S aints John and Barsanuphius lived in seclusion in a monastery, not far from Gaza, at the beginning of the sixth century. This did not prevent them from having a few followers and exercising a ministry of spiritual direction.

About the End of the World

A question from a monk was posed to Saint John of Gaza, "Tell me, Father, is the end of the world already set in an inescapable way?"

John answer, "Most certainly, the world will come to an end. But, if God is pleased with us, he will prolong time, because it is written (in Prov 10:27) 'The fear of the LORD prolongs life, but the years of the wicked will be short.'"

Correspondence Between Barsanuphius
and John of Gaza, Solesmes, 1993, p. 449.

Temptation

A monk asked a question of Saint Barsanuphius of Gaza, "Father, I am suffering from a flood of impure thoughts. How then can I be saved?"

Barsanuphius advised, "Brother, if you do not want to limp anymore, then pick up the cross as your walking stick!"

Correspondence Between Barsanuphius and John of Gaza, p. 86.

Saint Scholastica
Consecrated Virgin

Scholastica (approx. 480–543) was the sister of Saint Benedict (approx. 480–547), who was the Father of Western Monasticism. She spent her religious life at the foot of Monte Cassino where Benedict had founded his own religious community. Three days after their last meeting, Benedict had a vision of her soul flying to heaven as a dove.

Last Fraternal Meeting

Once a year, Benedict, accompanied by a few followers, went to visit his sister. This time, after having spent the day together in praise of God and in spiritual discussions, they had supper. Then, as it had become late, Scholastica said to her brother, Benedict, "I beg you, don't leave me tonight! Let us continue to speak throughout the night about the joys of life in heaven."

Benedict replied, "What are you asking, sister? There is no way I can live outside the monastery!"

Hearing these words, Scholastica put her hands together on the table and bowed her head to pray to God. A moment later, a violent storm began outside, preventing anyone from leaving. Very saddened, Benedict said to his sister, "May God forgive you, sister! What have you brought upon us?"

She replied to him, "I begged you and you would not hear. So, I prayed to God and He heard me. However, go ahead and leave, if you can!"

Benedict felt compelled to remain in spite of himself,

and in this way they were able to prolong their discussion about the spiritual life until morning."

Dialogues, Saint Gregory the Great, II, 33,
Patrologia Latina, J. P. Migne, t. 66, col. 194–6.

SAINT FRANCIS OF ASSISI
◆—
DEACON AND FOUNDER

Francis Bernardone was born in Assisi around 1182, and converted to a fervent Christian life in 1205. He founded the Order of the Friars Minor, which was approved by Pope Innocent III in 1209. He had a fruitful apostolic life, received the stigmata of Christ in 1224, and died on October 3, 1226, while singing Psalm 141. He was canonized in 1228.

AN INSISTENT HUMILITY

One day, Francis came before the Bishop of Imola in Romany to introduce himself, "Lord Bishop, I would like to have permission for my Brothers and I to preach in your diocese."

Brusquely, the Bishop replied, "My Brother, I myself preach to my people, that's enough!"

Francis bowed his head and left. An hour later, he returned. The Bishop asked him again, "What do you want, Brother? What permission have you come to ask of me again?"

"Lord," Francis answered, "when a father sends his son out one door, he must enter by another."

Won over by such an insistent humility, the Bishop said, "Henceforth, you and your Brothers may preach in my diocese: you have my permission, without reservation!"

Vita Secunda, Thomas de Celano, n. 147, trans. Br. Bernard Marie.

RESPECT FOR THE PRIESTHOOD

When he was crossing Lombardy, Francis entered a church to pray. The parish priest was giving scandal because he lived in a common-law marriage. A member of the Manichean sect said to Francis, "If a priest defiles himself with a concubine, can one still believe in his teachings and consider the sacraments he administers valid?"

Francis replied, "Sinful hands could not make my Lord impure, nor diminish His sacramental power. Out of respect for the Lord, I would then honor his ministry!" Having spoken in this manner, Francis went and bowed himself before the priest and kissed his hands.

Testimony of Étienne of Bourbon, Dominican (+1261), cited in
Documents (written), and the first Franciscan Biographies, Ed.
Franciscans: Paris, 1968–1981, p. 139.

A THWARTED TRAP

When Francis and the Enlightened Brother found themselves in the house of the Sultan of Egypt (in 1219), the Muslim ruler wanted to put Francis' Christian faith to the test. He spread a rug, decorated with designs in the form of a cross, on the ground and said to his assistants, "Bring this man who has the air of a true Christian to me. If he walks on the crosses of the rug, we will tell him that he has insulted his Lord. If he refuses to step forward, we will tell him that he has insulted us."

They called Francis. He crossed the rug from one end to the other and approached the Sultan, who said to Francis then, "You Christians, you revere the cross as a sacred sign and, meanwhile, you have trampled it underfoot!"

Francis replied, "Don't you know that we also crucified

thieves with Our Lord? We have the true cross and venerate it. To you, he has left the thieves' cross. That is why I did not hesitate to walk upon symbols of bandits."

"Testimony of the Enlightened Brother,"
cited in Documents, pp. 1331–1332.

An Example of Universal Brotherhood

One evening, Francis (already having the stigmata) was traveling along on the back of a donkey, accompanied by a Brother. Both arrived at the monastery at Saint Vergoin. Some peasants stopped them saying, "Go no further: some ferocious wolves are nearby. They could eat your donkey and you with it!"

"I did nothing wrong to my brother the wolf," replied Francis. "He wouldn't dare eat us. Good evening, my children, and believe in God!" Brother Francis and his companion continued along their way and no harm came to them.

"Anonymous Testimony of the Thirteenth Century,"
cited in Documents, p. 1347.

The Most Important Thing

Someone asked Francis one day what, according to him, seemed to be the most important thing. He replied, "Nothing is more important than saving souls! It is for these souls alone that the Son of God wished to die, and die on a cross."

Vita Secunda, Thomas de Celano, n. 172,
cited in Documents, p. 469.

The Only Consolation

One day when Francis was in pain, throughout his entire body, his companion said, "Father, would you like a reader to come read to you from the Scriptures for consolation?"

Replied Francis, "It's useless, my son, I know them well enough by now. My only consolation, from now on, is to better know Christ, poor and crucified!"

Vita Secunda, Thomas de Celano, n. 105,
cited in Documents, p. 412–413.

SAINT CLARE OF ASSISI
VIRGIN AND FOUNDER

S piritual friend and fellow countrywoman of Saint
Francis, Clare Offreduccio (1193–1253) founded the
"Poor Ladies (Clares)," which we later called the "Clarists."
Two years after her death, Pope Alexander IV canonized her.

HOW TO ANSWER SATAN

Often during prayer, Clare wept, her face on the ground.
One night, in the spot where she cried in this way, the angel
of darkness gave her the following warning, "Don't cry so
much, if you do, you'll go blind!"

She replied, "We are truly never blind, if we see God!"
The Life of Saint Clare, Thomas de Celano, §19,
trans. D. Vorreux, Ed. Franciscans: Paris, 1953, p. 37.

NO, NOT A SINGLE PRIVILEGE

Because of frequent problems in the region, Pope Gregory IX tried, one day, to persuade Clare to accept a few pieces
of property. The income from them would permit her, as
well as her Sisters, to no longer have to depend solely upon
public charity. The Pope added, "If your vow of poverty con-
stitutes the only obstacle preventing you from doing this, I
have the power to absolve you."

"Most Holy Father," she replied, "I could never allow it to
see myself absolved from the happiness of following Christ!"
The Life of Saint Clare, Thomas de Celano, §14, pp. 32–33.

SAINT LOUIS IX
KING OF FRANCE

The father of eleven children, born during thirty-six years of marriage, the "Baptized of Poissy" (as he was known), progressively became the Good King Saint Louis (1215–1270). His royal duties contributed to his sanctification, but he, himself, only wanted to follow the example of the King of Heaven: poor, just, and the servant of all.

THE DIGNITY OF THE BAPTIZED

One day, a lord of the royal court asked King Louis IX, "Sir, why do you always sign things as: Louis de Poissy?"

"It is really quite simple!" replied the King. "I respect the chapel where I was baptized even more than the cathedral where I was crowned."

Testimony of Guillaume de Nangis and de Joinville, cited, among others, in "People of the Saints," in Missel Hosanna, Trady: Paris, 1986, p. 328.

THE IMPORTANCE OF GIVING WITNESS IN THE ACT OF FAITH

One day, Louis IX asked his chronicler, Joinville, "Sénéchal, what was your father's name?"

"His name was Simon," Joinville answered.

"How do you know this?" queried the King.

"I think that I am sure because my mother told me."

"Then," replied the King, "you must firmly believe all of the articles of faith given as testimony by the apostles as you hear them sung each Sunday in the Credo!"

The History of Saint Louis, Jean Sire de Joinville, Desclée de Brouwer, nd, Catholic Faculty, Lille, p. 21.

SAINT THOMAS AQUINAS
DOCTOR OF THE CHURCH

He was a famous Italian Dominican (approximately 1225–1274) who taught theology, among other subjects in Paris. A man of prayer and reflection, Thomas produced a body of work, abundant and varied, notably, the *Summa Theologica*, which exerted a great influence on the thinking of the Church that endures even today.

THE HORROR OF FALSEHOOD

One day, a colleague asked Thomas, "Hurry, come look out the window, Brother Thomas: over there, it seems as if a cow is flying!"

Thomas, who approached said, "I see nothing."

Another colleague countered by saying, "You are a simpleton!"

Thomas replied seriously, "That is possible, but I would rather think that a cow could fly than think that a religious could lie."

Fioretti Thomistes, Guillaume de Tocco.

THE RELATIVITY OF THINGS

Brother Reginald, "Your Theological Summary, what a monument!"

Brother Thomas answered, "It seems to me that all I have written is just straw in comparison to what I have seen and was revealed to me.... The seed of things is far more preferable than the straw of words!"

Saint Thomas Aquinas, His Life, Guillaume de Tocco, trans. Pègues & Maquart, Paris, 1925, pp. 287–288.

SAINT LOUIS OF ANJOU
PRINCE AND BISHOP

The great-nephew of Saint Louis, he became a Franciscan at the age of sixteen, a bishop at twenty-two, and died the following year in the diocese of Aix-en-Provence (1274–1297).

AN EXAMPLE OF SELF-ABANDONMENT

On June 5, 1284, Louis' father, Charles II of Anjou, suffered a severe naval defeat at Naples. He was captured by the Aragonese fleet. The enemy agreed to his release in exchange for three of his sons, including Louis. This imprisonment lasted six long years. One day, one of his noble companions asked him, "How can you stay calm in a situation such as this?"

"To God's friends, adversity is more profitable than prosperity, " replied Louis.

His companion then asked, "In that case, could you perhaps stay a prisoner for life?"

"Why not," answered Louis, "if God wants it."

Saintliness Before the Age of Thirty,
J. Huscenot, Chalet: Paris, 1991, p. 82.

Saint Joan of Arc
<>
Patroness of France

Joan was born in Domrémy, in the Lorraine region, in 1412. From the age of thirteen, she had visions of the archangel Michael and offered herself totally to God. Later, at the age of seventeen, while watching her father's sheep, she heard supernatural voices which urged her to join the Dauphin Charles VII, heir to the throne of France, in forming an army and chasing the British out of France. She quickly enjoyed military success and soon made it possible for the King to be crowned at Reims. She was captured by the Burgundian forces, delivered to the British, judged by an ecclesiastical tribunal presided over by the Bishop of Beauvais, and condemned to burn at the stake as a heretic on May 31, 1431. Her cause was reviewed in 1456 and she was acquitted posthumously. She was canonized in 1920.

Joan Is Counseled From Above

In 1429, Joan and a small group of armed persons were escorting a convoy of provisions along the shore of the Loire River. One day, it became necessary to consider flushing the British out from their installations around the church at Saint Loup. John, the Count of Dunois, known as the Bastard of Orleans, hesitated to try such a show of force with so small a number of soldiers. Joan went to see him and said, "Are you the Bastard of Orleans?"

"Yes, I am," said John, "and I am happy to see you here." The Count continued, "Was it you who suggested I come here, onto this side of the river, and that I not continue on to where Talbot and the British are?"

Joan answered, "It was I, and others much wiser than I, who gave this advice, in the belief that we were doing what is better and safer. In the name of God, the advice of our Lord is wiser and more reliable than your own. You believed that I could mislead you, and it is you, above all, who is wrong, because I bring you better support than you could ever get from any soldier or any city: the support of the King of Heaven!"

Testimony of Dunois, in The Life and Death of Joan of Arc, Régine Pernoud, Hachette: Paris, 1953, pp. 129–130.

About Death

In August 1429, at the time of the entry of King Charles VII at Crépy-en-Valois, the Archbishop of Reims suddenly asked Joan, "Oh Joan, where do you hope to die?"

She responded, "Where it will please God, because I am neither sure of the time nor the place, any more than you are.... And if it pleases God my Creator, I would gladly retire now, put down my weapons, and go serve my mother and father by watching my lambs, along with my sister and brothers, who would rejoice so much to see me again!"

The Life and Death of Joan of Arc, Régine Pernoud, p. 137.

About Angels

Extracts of the minutes of the trial for condemnation (held in 1431):

Interrogator: "What form did Saint Michael take when he appeared to you?"

Joan: "I did not see him with a crown, and I know nothing about his clothes."

Interrogator: "Was he naked?"

Joan: "Do you believe that God has nothing with which to clothe him?"

Interrogator: "Did he have hair?"

Joan: "Why would anyone have cut it?" (...)

Interrogator: "Saint Michael and the other angels, were they with you a long time?"

Joan: "They appear many times among the Christians, but no one sees them, and I have seen them many times among the Christians."

The Spirituality of Joan of Arc, Régine Pernoud,
Mame: Paris, 1992, p. 56–58.

GOD AND THE CHURCH

Interrogator: "Do you wish to put all that you have done, good or bad, before the judgment of our Holy Mother Church?"

Joan: "With reference to the Church, I love it and I would like to support it with all my power for our Christian faith. And it is not I who should be prevented from going to Church and attending Mass."

Interrogator: "Would you like to submit what you have said and done to the judgment of the Church?"

Joan: "I submit to God, who sent me to our Lady and to all the saints in paradise. It seems to me that it is one and the same thing, the Church and God, and that should cause me no difficulty."

Interrogator: "Do you believe that you are subject to the Church of God which is on earth, that is to your lord the

Pope, the cardinals, archbishops, bishops, and other prelates of the Church?"

Joan: "Yes, God is served first!"

> *The Spirituality of Joan of Arc, Régine Pernoud, p. 82.*

ABOUT THE STATE OF GRACE AND PERSONAL SALVATION

The following passage is justifiably famous:

Interrogator: "Are you certain that you are in a state of grace?"

Joan: "If I am, may God keep me there! If I am not, may God put me there! I would be the unhappiest person in the world to not be there. If I was in a state of sin, the Voice (from heaven) would not come to me, I think. How I wish that the whole world could hear it as well as I do!"

Interrogator: "Why you rather than someone else?"

Joan: "It pleases God to do it this way, using a simple virgin to force the King's adversaries into defeat."

Interrogator: "Since your voices told you that you will go to the kingdom of paradise, do you believe your salvation to be a sure thing?"

Joan: "I firmly believe what my voices have told me: that I will be saved. I believe that so firmly, it is as if I am already there."

Interrogator: "There's a reply of great importance! But then, do you still need to confess anything?"

Joan: "I don't know if I have ever committed mortal sins, but if I was (actually) in a state of mortal sin, I think that Saint Catherine and Saint Margaret would immediately abandon me.... We could not clear our conscience too much!"

> *French Minutes of the Interrogation of Joan the Virgin,*
> *Paul Doncoeur, Melun, 1952.*

A SPONTANEITY FILLED WITH HUMOR

According to the testimony of Pierre Daron, Joan showed proof of an extraordinary memory during her trial, saying for example, "I already answered that eight days ago."

One day, however, one of the notaries, Boisguillaume, stood up to her. After verification, it was found that what Joan said was correct. She was very pleased and declared to the befuddled notary, "If you make another mistake, I will pull your ears!"

The Life and Death of Joan of Arc, Régine Pernoud, p. 213.

SAINT IGNATIUS OF LOYOLA
PRIEST AND FOUNDER

I gnatius was born in Spain. He converted to a faithful life at the age of thirty, became a priest at forty-seven and assumed the directorship of the religious Company he founded—the Jesuits—for fifteen years. He had an eventful life (1491–1556), going from a military career in the Spanish army to a studious and prayerful missionary existence in many countries of Europe.

ABOUT APOSTOLIC LIFE

When he was passing through Salamanca, Ignatius was asked by a Dominican under-prior, "About what subject do you preach?"

Ignatius explained, "In reality, we don't preach, but it does happen that we speak to some in a familiar way about certain things concerning God. We do this, for example, when we eat a meal together."

"Can you, all the same," persisted the under-prior, "give me an idea what you preach about?"

Replied Ignatius, "Sometimes we speak about one virtue, other times we speak about another by praising it. Or we speak about this or that vice by renouncing it."

The Story of a Pilgrim, Ignatius of Loyola, §65, in Writings, trans. Giuliani, DDB: Paris, 1991, p. 1052–1053.

PRISONER FOR LOVE

Doubting that people supposedly without culture could validly teach theology, some Dominicans of Salamanca imprisoned Ignatius and his companions. Francis de Mendoza went to visit them and asked Ignatius, "How are you doing and is it difficult for you to be imprisoned in this way?"

Answered Ignatius, "Do you think that prison is such a great hardship? Well, let me tell you that for the love of God, I would suffer much worse, if that was possible!"

The Story of a Pilgrim, §69, p. 1054–1055.

THE PRICE OF ONE SINGLE SOUL

Ignatius was hospitalized at the Magdalena hospital, near Loyola, for a few days. At that time, he decided to teach the catechism to the children there every day. His older brother, Martin, objected, "It is useless to trouble yourself with this, no one will come!"

Ignatius said, "Even if only one child comes, for me, that will be enough to justify my trouble."

After he had started to do it, many came to listen to him, even his brother!

The Story of a Pilgrim, §87–88, p. 1064–1065.

SAINT PHILIP NERI

PRIEST AND FOUNDER

Originally from Florence, Philip adopted Rome as his home (1515–1595). He was an excellent priest who devoted himself to the study of theology as well as to the service of his neighbors, notably the youth, the ill, and the prisoners. He founded a company of priests, the Congregation of the Oratory of Divine Love, which had as its goals: prayer, preaching, and parish ministry. He garnered the favor of many by his judgment and humor.

THE DAMAGING EFFECTS OF GOSSIP

One day, Philip said to one of his Roman penitents, "In penance, my girl, you will pluck a chicken while walking in the street. After that, you will turn around and go back on your tracks and pick up all the feathers which have fallen.

"All the feathers?" replied the girl. "But it is impossible, Father!"

"Well my girl," pointed out Philip, "it is also as impossible to take back all the damaging effects your gossip has seeded throughout the day!"

Biography, Countess Estienne d'Orves, Paris, 1895.

SPIRITUAL ADVICE

An Oratorian Father asked Philip Neri one day, "How can we best strive for perfection?"

Philip Neri answered, "It is best to adopt the habit of

defeating sin all the little events of life. One day, with the help of God, we will know how to defeat it in the big events."

Reported by Gallino in 1600.

A REASON TO ALWAYS REJOICE

One day, an Oratorian asked Philip, "Dear Father, how can we always be happy in the midst of our trials?"

"Well," advised Philip, "think about this: in heaven, the Virgin Mary is always next to God, and there she never stops praying for us!"

Life, P.G. Bacci.

SAINT ANDREW OF AVELLINO

PRIEST

An Italian priest and ecclesiastical lawyer at the age of twenty-four (1521–1608), Andrew abandoned the practice of law. His motive: the horror of reversals. He entered religious life with the Theatines and became an admirable spiritual director.

ABOUT VISITING THE SICK

A Theatine priest asked Andrew, "How long should one remain at the bedside of a sick person?"

To which Andrew replied, "Always be brief! There are two advantages to this: if they like you, they will be happy to see you come back. If you are boring, their displeasure will be brief."

Acta Sanctorum of November 10.

SAINT TERESA OF ÁVILA
VIRGIN, DOCTOR AND FOUNDRESS

Teresa of Ávila (1525–1582) entered the religious life with the Carmelites at the age of eighteen. In 1562, she founded her first reformed convent and never stopped founding more convents until her death. A great lady, she became a Doctor of the Church and an important author. The "Madre" was known for her candor.

THE TRIALS IN A CHRISTIAN LIFE

Teresa, while on a trip, hurt her leg. Turning to God, she said, "Lord, after so many problems, this is so badly timed!"

Replied God, "Don't you know that this is the way I treat my friends?"

"Well, Lord," responded Teresa, "I understand why you have so few!"

Humor of the Saints, J. Jacques, Bloud & Gay: Paris, 1938, p. 172.

ECCLESIASTICAL RESPONSIBILITIES AND HONORS

One day, someone asked this question of Teresa, "Would you like to ask God to let me know if I should accept or refuse this bishopric offered me? To assume this responsibility, will it be for His glory?"

"Lord God," asked Teresa, "what should I answer?"

In her prayers, Christ gave her this answer: "When he will clearly understand that the true exercise of power must be lived without any thought of ownership, then he will be able to accept this responsibility."

Life by Herself, Ch. 40, trans. P. Grégoire, Seuil: Paris, 1948, p. 470.

"In Medio Stat Virtus"

One day, someone offered some delicious grapes to Teresa and to Saint John of the Cross. Father John said, "If we thought about God's justice, we would never eat any of it!"

"Certainly," replied Teresa, "but if we thought of His goodness, we would always be eating it!"

Humor of the Saints, p. 130.

There Is a Time for Everything

One day, Teresa was eating at the same table with Don Michael de Marabès. They were serving partridge. The servant was surprised to see that a religious of her reputation would agree to be served such a meal. Teresa then said to her, "My dear, tell yourself this: when there are partridges, we eat partridges; and when it is time for penance, we do penance!"

Humor of the Saints, p. 27.

SAINT FRANCIS DE SALES
BISHOP, DOCTOR, FOUNDER

F rancis de Sales was from Thorens near Annecy (1567–
1622); he became a priest, then the Bishop of Geneva
in 1602. He founded the Visitation order, along with
Joan de Chantal. He is the Doctor of Christianity in the
French language. King Henry IV said of him, "That man from
Geneva has all the virtues and none of the faults. He is a rare
bird!"

THE PRE-EMINENCE OF CHARITY

Madame de Chantal said, "What rule of life do you pre-
scribe for me?"

Francis replied, "Do everything out of love and nothing
under duress. One must love obedience even more than fear-
ing disobedience. I leave you a spirit of freedom!"

Letter to Madame de Chantal, September 1604,
Complete Works, Annecy, 1902.

AN OBSTINATE FAULT

The president of Herse said, "When then does our ego
die?"

"Ego," answered Francis, "only dies with our body!"

Letter of July 7, 1620.

THE LIVES OF THE SAINTS

Msgr. Frémyot inquired, "The stories of the saints, can
we use them?"

Replied Francis, "But, my God, is there nothing so useful or so beautiful? It is the Gospel put into action!"

Letter to the Archbishop of Bourges.

SAINT ALOYSIUS GONZAGA

PATRON OF YOUTH

P rince of the Holy Empire, a Jesuit at seventeen, this gifted Italian died at the age of twenty-three (1568–1591). He is the patron saint of youth and religious novices.

ABOVE ALL, THE DUTY OF THE STATE

A young Jesuit saw Aloysius playing ball and said, "What would you do if, in the middle of your game, we tell you of your imminent death?"

"Well, I would continue to play," answered Aloysius.

Cited by Father Vergilio Cepari, first biographer of the saint.

LAST WORDS

From 1590 to 1591, Aloysius went to great lengths to provide service to the victims of the great plague which ravaged all of Italy. Struck by it himself, he prepared for his death on June 20, 1591. His Superior, Father Jean Carminata, visited him one last time. Aloysius told him, "I am leaving, Reverend Father!"

Father Carminata asked, "Where are you going?"

"To heaven, if my sins don't keep me away from it," answered Aloysius.

Exclaimed Father Carminata, "Look at that! Our Brother Aloysius speaks of going to heaven as if he is planning a walk to our country house in Frascati!"

Sainthood Before the Age of Thirty, J. Huscenot, Chalet: Paris, 1991, p. 89.

Saint Rose of Lima

Consecrated Virgin

Rose Flores was born in Lima, Peru (1586–1617), the eleventh child of Gaspard, a retired soldier from a wealthy Spanish family from Puerto Rico, and Marie Oliva, a native of Lima. Times changed their fortune and the family found themselves living in poverty. Her baptismal name was Isabelle, but her parents called her Rose, because of her beauty.

She was a precocious child, the Holy Spirit touched her at an early age (nine months). She was also a joyful child, devoting her life totally to God at five, taking a vow of virginity, mortifying herself, and doing penance. She devoted herself to helping the poor, taking them food and, at night, sewing to support her family. The Lord appeared to her often, telling her of his pleasure at her kind deeds to the poor.

Rose died at the age of thirty-one. She is the first saint of the Americas, canonized in 1671.

About Suffering

When she was just a child of three, Rose was afflicted with a type of leprosy, principally on her head. At that time, the only known treatment was the application of mercury which, while treating the affected areas, also destroyed the surrounding flesh. She was in tremendous pain, even to the point of convulsions, yet she didn't complain. Her mother asked her, "Rose, how can you endure such pain, such torment?"

Rose, at first, said nothing, but turning toward her crucifix, replied, "The pain of the crown of thorns was much worse!"

37

In took forty-two more days of the same torment before she was completely healed.

Saint Rose of Lima, Patron of the New World, A. L. Masson, Classic and General Catholic Books: Lyons, 1898, p. 40.

BEAUTY

Rose was very beautiful and her mother wanted to dress her in beautiful clothes. Rose refused and said, "Mother, only the beauty of the soul is important!"

Book of Saints, L.G. Lovasik, S.V.D., Catholic Book Publishing: New York, 1981, p. 21.

OBEDIENCE

Rose had a strict sense of obedience; she sought out opportunities to practice it, as she was drawn to it. She prayed each morning that her mother would patiently explain to her the tasks of the day, but her mother found this bothersome and one day she said, impatiently, "Rose, do you take me for your servant? Can't you leave me alone? Attend to your duties yourself!"

Rose humbly replied, "I am sorry, Mother, my work is such a small thing. I will use it as a sign of my obedience. I will be more discrete in my requests."

A few days later, on the same subject, her mother wondered if Rose's spirit of obedience came from a sense of humility and to what length Rose would exercise it. As Rose was embroidering a stole, she complained, "You aren't doing it correctly, you must hold the material this way and put your needle in the other way."

Rose, knowing that this method suggested by her mother would produce disastrous results, nonetheless obeyed without question. A few days later, upon inspection of Rose's work, her mother commented, "Rose, look at the flowers, they're backwards! This is a total mess! Either you are sleeping on the job, or you're stupid!"

Rose gently replied, "In spite of my own lack of taste, like you, I find these flowers ridiculous! I could do nothing about it since I didn't want to stray from the new method you showed me earlier. I prefer to obey you than follow my own better judgment! I am ready to redo it, if you ask me to."

Saint Rose of Lima, Patron of the New World, p. 49–50.

THE WILL OF GOD

Rose adopted the habit of the Third-order Dominicans in spite of her mother's efforts to get her to marry. The Archbishop of Lima of the time had a friend, Marie de Quinones, who had just founded a Clarist convent. Marie offered Rose, on the Archbishop's recommendation, the opportunity to enter her order and become one of the first novices. Their vows of austerity, virginity, firmness against vices, and closeness to the Beloved was very attractive to Rose, as she was already practicing these herself. She wanted to join them and felt that her Mother wouldn't dare oppose the Archbishop's recommendation. She was wrong, her mother did oppose and gave her two reasons: the family, now extremely poor, needed Rose's work to support them; and they needed Rose to care for her oldest sibling, who was crippled. Torn between these two worlds, she prepared in secret, on the advice of her confessor, to enter the convent.

One day, Rose left to visit the convent with the firm conviction never to return home. Accompanied by one of her brothers, she asked him to let her stop to pray at the parish church, which was on the way. He agreed. Rose entered and kneeled at the Chapel of the Rosary, asking the Blessed Virgin Mary to intercede to change her parents' minds. All at once Rose felt her legs stiffen and it seemed as if she was cemented to the ground, she couldn't move. Her brother came to get her as time was quickly wasting away. Her legs were like marble, she couldn't move. Her brother tried to lift her three times to no avail. He was afraid that her plan would be discovered. Turning to the Blessed Virgin and her Son, she asked, "I asked God to tell me of his will. It must be that he wants me to return home to my family and not enter the convent."

To Mary, she said, "I promise that if you release me, I'll go home and wait until you tell me to leave."

All at once she felt her legs return to normal, she got up easily and returned home. Having to face her mother and explain her long absence, she simply said, "God sent me home, I now know his will. When God is consulted sincerely, he gives a clear answer!"

Saint Rose of Lima, Patron of the New World, p. 75–77.

A MARRIAGE MADE IN HEAVEN

Throughout her life, Rose had many mystical experiences with the Blessed Virgin Mary and our Lord. One day when she was in front of a statue of the Blessed Virgin who was holding the baby Jesus, she heard Jesus speak to her, "Rose of my heart, marry me."

Amazed, yet respectful in her belief, taken back by this, Rose found it impossible to reply at first. Her joy overflowed and finally she replied, "I am your servant, Lord…this is more than I dared hope for…I am yours now and for all eternity."

Then Mary said, "You can see, my daughter, the rare

honor Jesus has deemed to bestow upon you, taking you as his wife. Could he prove his love for you any better?"

The secret of this marriage was not known until after Rose's death.

Saint Rose of Lima, Patron of the New World, p. 142–143.

ABOUT HER DEATH

Rose fell ill and was accepted into the home of her friend Marie de la Massa, who cared for her. The Lord appeared to her, telling her that she would suffer a great deal. Accepting this with love, she explained to her friend, "I will leave this life in four months, at that time my soul will rise to be with my Beloved. I will die here with you. If, by chance I become incapacitated while visiting my family, don't worry, I won't die there!"

Shortly thereafter, she contracted pleurisy. She suffered incredibly. Dying, she said, "Heavenly Doctor, use my blood to wash away my sins."

Later that evening, while Father Lorenzana was standing vigil at her bedside, he prepared to leave for the night, thinking she would last until the morning. Bidding her goodbye, with a blessing, he said. "I must go now, I have to return to the convent. I'll see you in the morning."

Rose, knowing of the exact time of her death, answered with a smile, "Don't go yet. If you wait until morning, I will be far away! I have already received my invitation; at midnight, when the feast of Saint Barthelemy begins, that is when the doors of heaven will open to me."

Saint Rose of Lima, Patron of the New World, p. 305, 312, 319.

At the exact time she gave to the priest, Rose became serene, a look of joy came over her. Making the Sign of the Cross, she looked up to heaven, repeated "Jesus, be with me" three times, and died. In death, she regained her once famous beauty. The ravages of the fever disappeared completely, her skin shined brightly, and a smile appeared on her lips.

Saint Vincent de Paul
Priest and Founder

H e was born near Dax (1581–1660) and became a priest at twenty. Deeply touched by the misery of the people, he was involved in a variety of charity work. Preacher of missions and retreats, in 1625, he gathered a group of priests together in a new institute, the Congregation of the Mission, later called the Lazarists. From 1635 on, he helped Louise de Marillac organize the Sisters of Charity.

Tact for the Tactless

During a trial with a tactless benefactor, who had, among other things, damaged his reputation, Vincent stated that he did not want a single transcript to contain any aggressive words about the plaintiff. Someone said to him, "But Sir, you see what he says against you, and he even gives false statements!"

"That is not important," replied Vincent de Paul. "One must endure it! Our Lord suffered much more. (…) The Good Lord wants us to carry on."

M. Vincent, Told by his Secretary, A. Dodin, OEIL: Paris, 1991, p. 137.

Seek Simplicity in All Things

During a chapter meeting, a member of the Company confessed to having used dubious words in the course of a meeting. Vincent made this comment: "Whoever does not act in a simple manner, but quite to the contrary, uses questionable words, imitates the devil. (…) One must avoid questionable situations like the devil, even more so, since they ruin the spirit of simplicity which must shine in this Company."

M. Vincent, Told by his Secretary, p. 57.

ALL THE SAME, A CONSOLATION

B. Condoing, a priest with the Company, asked Vincent, "Do you have any consolation?"

Saint Vincent de Paul replied, "The consolation which our Lord gives me is that I always work to follow, and not avoid, Providence."

Letter of May 14, 1644.

WORDS OF CHRIST ON THE CROSS

A listener asked, "What did Jesus say on the cross?"

Vincent exclaimed, "Five statements, and not one of them expressed impatience!"

Spiritual Conversations.

ABOUT THE VIRTUE OF JOY

One day, the Counsel of the Sisters of Charity asked the following question of Vincent, "What must one do to show a happy face when the heart is sad?"

He answered, "I tell you, it is not important if your heart is full of joy or not, as long as your face shows happiness. This isn't covering up the truth, because the charity you have for your Sisters is in the will. If you have the will to please them, it will be enough to make your face show joy. It is in this way, my Daughters, that virtues are acquired. If everyone showed their disagreeable feelings, you would see some unbelievable expressions!"

The Complete Works of Saint Vincent de Paul,
Gabalda: Paris, 1920–1925, t. IX, p. 150.

SAINT JOHN BERCHMANS

JESUIT

John was born near Brussels (1599–1621) and entered the Maline Jesuits at the age of seventeen. He was sent to Rome for his novitiate and died at the age of twenty-two. His faithfulness to their code of conduct was of heroic proportions, and he was later chosen to be the patron of Mass servers.

THE LITURGY OF THE PRESENT MOMENT

In August 1621, John was afflicted with severe dysentery. His condition quickly became critical, and his nurse thought it necessary to warn him, "Brother John, I believe that you have only a few days to live. I am deeply saddened by this."

She continued, asking, "Don't you have any worries at the prospect of appearing before God?

"Absolutely none!"

A few days later, John's father came to visit him and said, "Dear son, may our Lord give both of us a saint's death!"

John answered, "Certainly, Father, but isn't it necessary for us to live as saints first?"

"How, then, can we achieve that?" asked his father.

Counseled John, "One must live only for the here and now. We must seek to go to heaven at each and every moment!"

Sainthood Before the Age of Thirty, J. Huscenot,
Chalet: Paris, 1991, p. 77–78.

SAINT MARGARET MARY ALACOQUE
CONSECRATED VIRGIN

Margaret Mary Alacoque (1647–1690) was born in Burgundy, entered the Visitation order at Paray-le-Monial in 1671, and was made aware of a variety of different revelations from Christ. During the last revelation, in June 1675, he showed her the open wounds on his side, telling her, "This is the Heart that so loved mankind!" Margaret Mary, assisted by Father Claude La Colombière, worked to spread public and liturgical devotion to the Sacred Heart of Christ, which proved to be a providential response to the errors of Jansenism, which was very strong at the time.

DIALOGUE LIKE ABRAHAM

In a vision she had around 1675, Margaret Mary had an astonishing conversation with Christ. Their conversation was somewhat reminiscent of the dialogue that Abraham had with God on the subject of the sinful city of Sodom (See also Gn 18:17–32). In the dialogue with Margaret Mary, Christ confided his sorrow to the religious about the impending deaths of certain people around her. Learning this, she quickly reacted, "Oh my Savior, instead, levy your justice on me,… but don't let those souls which cost you so dearly go to waste!"

Christ countered, "They don't love you and won't ever stop afflicting you."

Margaret Mary replied, "That isn't important, my Lord, as long as they love you!"

"Let me do as I wish! I can't stand them any longer," said the vision.

"No, my Lord," pleaded Margaret Mary, "I will not relent until you have forgiven them!"

"All right," replied the Lord, "as long as you agree to answer for their behavior."

"Yes, my Lord," promised Margaret Mary, "but I will always repay you only with your own riches, which are the treasures of your Sacred Heart!"

The Life of Margaret Mary Alacoque,
Saint Paul: Paris, 1979, p. 136.

SAINT JOHN BAPTIST DE LA SALLE
PRIEST AND FOUNDER

During a life that encompassed sixty-eight years (1651–1719), this brilliant professor wanted to democratize the schools. A French priest, the product of a learned background, he founded a nonsacerdotal congregation, the Brothers of the Christian Schools. His religious schoolmasters would, in a Christian school setting, join together both religious vocations and trades, to produce a vital harmonious synthesis.

A HUMBLE VOCATION BUT SO VERY USEFUL!

Certain well-intentioned persons were amazed that John Baptist de La Salle, himself being a priest, wanted to found an institute for religious lay people. They said, "Sir, the members of your institute do not celebrate at the altar, consecrate the flesh, hear confessions, or celebrate baptisms. Isn't this bad for the Church and for the glory of God?"

This man of God normally answered this type of question using the same words he used to address his young novices and those professed in the faith: "If your duties do not put the censer into your hands to offer incense to the Almighty in the temple, at least you have the honor to prepare living temples for him and to work towards the sanctification of those young people who have been forgotten by society. If there are more honorable ministries in the Church, there are few more useful. We see enough religious brothers and monks, but not enough catechists, destined by their faith and vocation to instruct the young people. It is by teaching Christian doctrine that you act as apostles…. Saint Paul made this his primary goal: he, himself, declared that heaven had sent him to evangelize and teach Christian doctrine."

The Life of the Venerable Servant of God, John Baptist de La Salle,
Jean-Baptiste Blain, Procure Générale de Paris, 1887, p. 446–447.

PRAYER AND CONFIDENCE

During the great Paris famine of 1709, the supplies of the community were found to be depleted. John Baptist de La Salle remained calm and left it all in God's hands. The following morning, on his way to say Mass, he met a person who asked, "Sir, may I know where you are going?"

"I am going to celebrate holy Mass, and pray to God that He send our community what we need to survive the day as we have no food and foresee none coming," replied John.

Touched by his words, the person replied, "Go in peace: I will provide for you myself." That person kept his word, sending money to the community, satisfying the pressing need.

The Life of the Venerable Servant of God,
John Baptist de La Salle, p. 617.

LAST WORDS

Brother Barthélemy said, "Dearest Father, do you happily accept the sorrows you suffer?"

Dying, John Baptist de La Salle replied, "I adore the way God has treated me in all things!"

The Life of Saint John Baptist de La Salle, Jean Guibert,
Librarie Poussielgue: Paris, 1901, p. 612.

Saint Louis Grignion de Montfort
PRIEST AND FOUNDER

A Breton native, born in 1673 in Montfort-sur-Meu (Ille-de-Vilaine), he died in 1716 at Saint-Laurent-sur-Sèvres (Vandée), Louis was a dauntless rural preacher. He evangelized in five French provinces: Brittany, Anjou, Poitou, Normandy, and Saintonge. He founded many institutes, notably the Missionaries of the Company of Mary and the Sisters of Divine Wisdom.

A Poor Person at the Door

Father Louis stopped for a moment at the Fontevrault Abbey where his sister Sylvia and other religious lay people lived. The Sister at the door said, "Who are you, Sir?"

Louis replied, "That is not important, I ask for charity, for the love of God."

The Sister was impressed with the humility and gentleness of this poor person. She sent for the Mother Abbess, who, in turn, asked, "Who are you, then?"

"Madam, my name is unimportant. It is not for myself that I ask for charity, but for the love of God."

A moment later, not having been able to get any satisfaction, Father Louis moved away, still unrecognized. The incident was reported to Sister Sylvia, who recognized her brother from the description given to her. The Sisters ran to find the priest and, with many explanations, begged him to return. He then responded, "Mother Abbess refused to give me charity for the love of God. Now, she offers it to me for my own sake. I thank her, but I will seek help elsewhere, from the poor!"

Louis Grignion de Montfort, T. Rey-Mermet,
Nouvelle Cité: Paris, 1984, p. 74–75.

STRENGTH OF SOUL WHEN PUT TO THE TEST

Pierre des Bastières came to Louis to support him through the difficulties he was encountering: the destruction (by order of the Bishop) of the beautiful crucifix he had built, some fifteen months prior, near Pont-Château. Finding the priest very calm, he was surprised, "Are you comfortable with the fact that they destroyed your crucifix?"

Louis Grignion de Montfort replied, "I am neither comfortable with that, nor angry. The Lord allowed me to have it built; today, He allows it to be destroyed. May His holy name be blessed! If it was up to me, it would remain until the end of time, but, as it is up to God now, may His holy will be done, and not my own!"

Lifting his hands and eyes towards heaven, the priest said aloud:

"I would prefer, my Lord, to die a thousand times than to go against your holy will!"

Louis Grignion de Montfort, p. 95.

SAINT MARGUERITE D'YOUVILLE

FOUNDRESS

Marguerite Lajemmerais d'Youville (1701–1771) was the first saint to be born on Canadian soil. She was raised in a well-to-do family, just outside of Montreal. Her father was a career soldier from France of a certain renown who died when she was seven years old. Marguerite's family arranged her marriage, when she was twenty-one, to François d'Youville, a man of dubious dealings in illegal liquor. She had six children, two of whom survived the rigors of life in the colony. After eight years of marriage, she became a widow.

The eighteenth century was not an ideal time for a woman to seek a change in lifestyle. Boundaries were set in stone by society, any deviations were scorned upon. In spite of this, Marguerite sought to change life for the ill and homeless of Montreal and embark on a spiritual journey of her own. She began a lay organization called the Confraternity of the Holy Family, whose goal was the care and visitation of the ill, the lonely, the homeless, and the orphans. She truly wished to found a religious order for women, but at that time, it would have had to be a cloistered order, which would defeat her purposes. She was given a home for her charges and also appointed Director of the General Hospital in Montreal, in spite of not receiving any support from the Governor and the Bishop. Taking secret vows, she and three other devoted women pursued their chosen apostolate, until some years later they were granted permission to found the religious order we now call the Grey Nuns or the Grey

Sisters of Charity, an order that was "of the world," wearing simple grey or black dresses and no veil (feeling that a veil would separate them from the world or prevent them from seeing it as it really was).

In spite of great controversy, she also ministered to the Native peoples. She was canonized in 1990, a woman devoted to the Holy Family, seeking to find them on earth in the global family, regardless of age, sex, color, or nation of origin.

WHEN YOU LACK THE ESSENTIALS

Marguerite, a widow with two sons to raise, was penniless and had lost her home, due to the criminal activities of her late husband. She was more determined than ever to pursue her work in the Confraternity. The following is a recount of her convictions about charity, when she was asked, "Madam, when one lacks the essentials of life, how can one possibly give to the Church and the poor?"

Marguerite replied, "My answer is that if you lack the essentials, it's because you have not given enough to others! our Lord said: 'give and you will receive.' I tell you, if you have little, give little, but if you have a great deal, give a great deal. And whatever you give, do it generously. You sow so little to reap infinitely."

Mother d'Youville, Albertine Ferland-Angers,
Beauchemin: Montreal, 1945, p. 61.

FIRM CONVICTIONS

In among her many business letters, we find a few jewels of a personal nature. To her friend, Madame de Blainville, she wrote, "Tomorrow, we will say a Mass for the cure of your leg. I am sure that it is already healed by now and you won't need it, but with God, nothing is lost."

This phrase, "With God, nothing is lost," was her trademark, her anthem, her very foundation, and the entire basis of her faith.

Mother d'Youville, p. 180.

A BUSINESS WOMAN, A STRONG WOMAN

In May 1765, her first "home" for her patients burned to the ground. The source of the fire was then, and still is to this day, of a suspicious nature.

The building was destroyed almost totally, except for a single cornerstone. Mother d'Youville wrote to her friend, Madam de Lignery, about it: "The wind was horrible and carried the flames directly to us (at 2:30 A.M.).... We were mere ashes in minutes.... We have moved the patients over to the main hall of the hospital (Hotel Dieu). As for us, I know that we are hardy enough to withstand living outside, next to the cornerstone which is still standing. It is as strong as our faith."

She continued, "I am sorry to report that your beautiful dress was destroyed as well with many others.... We have found some money that was burned. I will have it cleaned and try to sell it, so we haven't lost everything!

"François Lamarche died two days after the fire as a result of his injuries. He hadn't yet paid his rent.... I think I will ask his brother for it!"

Mother d'Youville, p. 227.

THE PASSION FOR GOODNESS

After Mother d'Youville's death in 1771, the Quebec Gazette published the following biographical note, written by Father Desjardins:

"She was devoured with the passion for goodness, consumed with it..., doing all she could, without ever seeking it, yet never giving up. Her religious zeal was brilliant (as a light) and untiring. She was a woman of many talents: she could change people's minds to a degree that would seem impossible, yet she did it subtly; she had a keen sense of foresight...."

In reply to this, the Vicar General and Superior of the major seminary in Quebec City, Jerome Demers, wrote, in a letter to Jacques Viger, "We can truly say with a clear and sure conscience that there was no exaggeration in the biographical notes written by Father Desjardins in the Quebec Gazette. It all perfectly conforms to the truth!"

Mother d'Youville, p. 358.

SAINT SERAPHIM OF SAROV
PRIEST AND SPIRITUAL MASTER

Born in Kursk, Russia (1759–1833), he entered the monastery at Sarov at the age of nineteen, was ordained a priest, and spent some thirty years as a hermit in the forest. Following this, he cloistered himself in a cell of the same monastery for five years. His reputation as a spiritual master was common knowledge, and people came from far and wide to consult him about a variety of problems. This renown followed him even after death, he who had said, "When I am gone, come to my tomb and I will help you!" He was canonized by the Russian Church in 1903.

THE VIRTUE OF JOY

A religious asked Father Seraphim, "Is joy a form of misbehavior, hence, a sin?"

"No, little mother," advised Seraphim, "just the opposite! Joy chases away fatigue, because out of fatigue comes discouragement, there is nothing worse!… Certainly, in the house of God, it is improper to speak or to misbehave, but a kindly, joyful, encouraging word is not a sin. It could help a person's spirit to remain joyful before God."

Séraphim of Sarov, trans. I. Gorainoff,
Abbaye de Bellefontaine, 1973, p. 16–17.

HOW TO DETECT THE HOLY SPIRIT

On September 9, 1831, a young Russian nobleman, Nicolas Motovilov, asked Father Seraphim, "Father, you always say that the goal of a Christian life is to welcome the

Holy Spirit into our hearts. But how can I recognize that whatever is happening is from Him?"

Replied Seraphim, "The Holy Spirit himself attests to his presence. Actually, we are both filled with the bounty of the Holy Spirit. Look at me!"

The young nobleman protested, "I can't, Father. Your face has become as bright as the sun!"

"Do not be afraid!" answered Seraphim, "You, yourself, have also become as bright as I. You are also in the bounty of the Holy Spirit, otherwise you could see nothing. Dare to look at me without fear because God is with us. The Lord taught us this: '...the kingdom of God is among you' (Lk 17:21). By the kingdom of God, He meant the grace of the Holy Spirit. This is the state we find ourselves now in, actually it is what he had in mind when he promised his disciples that some of them would see the kingdom of God which 'has come with power'" (Mk 9:1).

Séraphim of Sarov, Discussion With Motovilov, p. 125–127.

HOW TO MAKE PROGRESS IN THE UNION WITH GOD

On another occasion, Nicolas Motovilov again questioned Saint Seraphim on the same subject, which is crucial in spiritual life: "Father, how can I know if the Holy Spirit is always with me?"

"If he is with you," Seraphim answered, "may God be blessed! Then, you don't have to worry, even if the final day of judgment was tomorrow. But if, on the other hand, you are no longer certain that you are with the Holy Spirit, it is necessary to discover the reason why he abandoned you. In effect, it is necessary for you to hunt the enemies down, who are preventing you from going to God, without giving up, all the way to the point of their complete annihilation....

"You can recognize the work of the Holy Spirit in the deeds he does in memory of the teachings of Christ, in the work he does in conjunction with him to guide our steps along the path of peace. With regard to the diabolical spirit, he incites us to revolt: he makes us slaves to the flesh, vanity, and pride. Finally, do not forget that, at the side of the Son of God, you have a tireless lawyer, an invincible litigant for the most hardened sinners. That is why Mary, the Mother of God, was called 'the devil's curse': no demon could ever cause a person to perish as long as they continuously sought the help of 'Theotokos.'"

Seraphim of Sarov, Discussion with Motovilov, p. 193–204.

SAINT ELIZABETH ANN SETON
WIDOW AND FOUNDRESS

lizabeth Bayley (1774–1821), the charming daughter of a doctor from Baltimore, married at the age of nineteen. She and her husband, William Seton, a rich businessman, had three daughters and two sons. A confessed Episcopalian, she converted to Catholicism in 1805, two years after the death of her husband. Her last sixteen years of earthly life were particularly active and prayerful: a pedagogical and religious career founding seven teaching and charitable congregations. She was the first American saint, canonized September 14, 1975.

THE MEANING OF THE CHURCH

As Mother Seton lay dying, a religious asked, "Mother, what is your final advice?"

Replied Mother Seton, "I have told you often: be daughters of the Church!"

Dear Remembrance, Msgr. Robert, New York, 1869.

BLESSED ANNE MARIE JAVOUHEY
VIRGIN AND FOUNDRESS

A native of Burgundy, she lived to the age of seventy-two (1779–1851), through the French Revolution, the First Empire, the two Restorations, and the Second Republic. In the midst of these dynamic national events, this noble lady was openly preoccupied with international events. She was the foundress of the Sisters of Saint Joseph of Cluny and is known as an exceptional person and one of the first women missionaries.

THE VIRTUE OF PEACE

A Sister of Saint Joseph said to her, "In spite of my efforts, I am still anxious and fearful. How can I stop this?"

Mother Javouhey replied, "I find you despondent, discontent, I could almost say barely charitable. My God, why do you torment yourself in this way? Do you believe you can do good? No, no, you are mistaken! Keep your soul peaceful! Don't ever trouble yourself with the bad things that aren't your fault: you will do infinitely more good if you would be calmer!"

Journal of a Lady, An Apostle of Faraway Places,
album "Univers media," 1979, p. 18.

SAINT JOHN VIANNEY
PRIEST, CURÉ OF ARS

Born near Lyon, he entered his priestly studies at the age of nineteen and, in spite of a difficult apprenticeship in Latin, was ordained in 1815. His bishop, Msgr. Devie, then stated, "He is perhaps not very educated, but in any event, he is enlightened!" He was named the Curé of Ars in 1818 and remained there until his death (1786–1859). He often spent up to eighteen hours a day in the confessional and assisted in the blessing of the large crowds who came to see him from far and wide. One day, a lady possessed with the devil confessed, "Oh, how you make me suffer! If there were three like you on earth, my kingdom would be destroyed!"

A SAINTLY CONFESSOR

Father Dubois, parish priest of Fareins (six kilometers from Ars) asked Father Vianney one day, "We hear that you give light penance to great sinners?"

The saintly priest replied, "The confessor also has to do his part!"

John Vianney, Curé of Ars, Abbey Nodet,
Xavier Mappus: Le Puy, 1960, p. 105.

ABOUT THE LOUDNESS OF HIS VOICE

One day, a person made this observation to the saintly priest: "Father, why is it that when you pray, we barely hear you, but when you preach, you speak so loudly?"

The Curé answered, "The reason is that when I preach, I often speak to the deaf or to people who are sleeping, but when I pray, I am dealing with God, and God is not deaf!"

John Vianney, Curé of Ars, p. 128.

ABOUT THE MERCY OF GOD

A pilgrim who came to Ars remarked, "I have done too many bad things. God could not forgive me!"

To this, Father Vianney replied, "To speak in this manner is blasphemy. It is putting a road block on God's mercy, and there are none: His mercy is infinite!"

John Vianney, Curé of Ars, p. 149.

ABOUT REPENTANCE

One day, a penitent person expressed surprise to Father Vianney, asking, "Why are you crying?"

Father Vianney explained, "Oh, my friend, I cry about those things that you don't cry about!"

John Vianney, Curé of Ars, p. 144.

Another time, a desperate widow came to Ars because her husband had committed suicide by throwing himself into the river, and she feared for his eternal salvation. On the road to the vicarage, she came across Father Vianney. He looked at her and declared, bending towards her, "He is saved!"

As she made a gesture of disbelief, the priest added, "I tell you, that he is saved! He is in purgatory and we must pray for him. Between the parapet of the bridge and the water, he had the chance to make an act of contrition. It is the Blessed Virgin who gave him this grace. Remember your special prayers during the month of Mary. Even as he had often not been religious, your husband was, at times, united with you in prayer. That is what earned him penance and the supreme pardon."

The Life of the Curé of Ars, Msgr. Trochu, Vitte: Lyon, 1929, p. 631.

THE HUMILITY OF A SAINT

Catherine Lassagne, the sexton of Ars, had commented that Father Vianney often appeared to suffer from great inner sadness. One day, when she saw him particularly afflicted, she said to him, "You must wish to withdraw because you have too much sadness!"

John Vianney responded, "Sadness is nothing! I cry about my poor life and prepare myself for death."

John Vianney, Curé of Ars, p. 204.

HIS LOVE OF THE IMMACULATE VIRGIN

A little after the proclamation of the dogma of the Immaculate Conception by Pope Pius IX (1854), someone asked Father Vianney, "What do you think of the proclamation of the new dogma?"

"What happiness!" the Curé commented. "I always thought that we were missing one ray in the sunburst of Catholic truths. It was a gap that could not be left open in our religion."

John Vianney, Curé of Ars, p. 256.

NEARING HIS DEATH

On the 11 of May, 1843, afflicted with pleurisy, the Saint of Ars appeared close to death. Seven priests were assembled in his room and one of them suggested, "It would no doubt be good if you could receive Extreme Unction, but it will have to be without the ringing of the bells, so as to not discourage the pilgrims."

To this, Father Vianney replied, "Yes, yes, ring them! A priest always needs someone to pray for him."

Some years later, on the 29 of July, 1859, when he was dying, the Notary of Trévoux came to ask him, "Father, where would you like to be buried?"

Answered Father Vianney, "In Ars...but my body is nothing special!"

The Curé of Ars and His Passion, La Varende,
Chalet: Paris, 1986, p. 160, 219.

BLESSED JEANNE JUGAN
VIRGIN, FOUNDRESS

A native of Breton, she was born in Cancale (1792–1879) into a family of poor seafarers. She spent eight years caring for the sick at the hospital in Saint Servan. Around 1835, she began to welcome elderly women, the poor, the sick, and the homeless into her own home. As a result, she founded the congregation of the Little Sisters of the Poor, which was recognized by Rome in 1854.

PATIENCE ABOVE ALL THINGS

One day, when Jeanne was taking a collection, without wanting to, she apparently annoyed an elderly bachelor. He slapped her face. She calmly answered him, "Thank you, that was for me! Now, if you please, give me a donation for the poor!"

Jeanne Jugan, Paul Milcent,
De la Tour Saint Joseph, 1982, p. 22.

HOW TO HANDLE DISAGREEMENTS

One day, a novice asked Jeanne, "Sister, how do we act when someone says something disagreeable to us?"

"You must act like a bag of wool which, when a rock is tossed in, it deadens the sound," answered Jeanne.

Jeanne Jugan, p. 55.

THE DIVINE SCULPTOR

One day, Jeanne called a young Sister to come to the open window. She showed her the stonemasons who were cutting stones outside, saying, "Do you see these workers who are cutting the white stone for the chapel, and how they are making that stone beautiful? Well, my little one, let yourself be cut in the same way by our Lord!"

Jeanne Jugan, p. 56.

THE CHRISTIAN LIFE, A LIFE OF LOVE

One day, while passing in front of a garden of flowers, Jeanne pointed out a particularly beautiful flower to a young Sister and asked, "Do you know who made that?"

"It is God's handiwork!" answered the young Sister.

Jeanne fixed her gaze at it and added with wonder, "Even more than that. He who is our Husband made it!"

Jeanne Jugan, p. 57.

WHAT TO THINK ABOUT INTROSPECTION

A novice from Saint Pern one day asked Jeanne, "Mother, must I again go inside of myself to better know myself?"

"No, my daughter!" answered Jeanne. "All that is necessary is for you to turn toward God and throw yourself totally into Him!"

Souvenirs of the Novitiate, July 1879.

WARNING TO YOUNG PEOPLE

One day, Jeanne, then aged eighty-four, said to a few novices who were gathered around her, "When you're old, you will see nothing. Me, I see nothing other than God!"

Jeanne Jugan, Humble for Love,
P. Milcent, Centurion: Paris, 1978, p. 216.

LAST WORDS

On August 28, 1879, she was heard praying just a few moments before her departure for heaven, "Eternal Father, open Your doors today, to the most destitute of Your little daughters, but one who has the greatest desire to see You!... O Mary, my good Mother, come to me! You know that I love you and I have such a great desire to see you!"

Then, right after these words, she slipped gently away.

Jeanne Jugan, Humble for Love, p. 228.

SAINT CATHERINE LABOURÉ
CONSECRATED VIRGIN

B orn in Côte d'Or (1806–1876), she entered the Sisters of Charity in 1830. She humbly devoted her entire life in service to the poor, mainly the elderly and the ill. When she was at the convent on the Rue du Bac in Paris, she experienced several apparitions of our Lady. Most notably, the Blessed Virgin asked her to have a medal struck with the inscription: "O Mary, conceived without sin, pray for us who have recourse to you."

NOT A STATIONARY IMAGE, BUT A LIVING APPARITION

Around 1874, a young Sister found herself not far from Sister Catherine while she was relaxing. All at once, she exclaimed, in a provocative tone, "She who saw her, only saw a painting!"

Immediately, Catherine straightened up saying, "My dear, the Sister who saw the Blessed Virgin, saw her in the flesh, like you and I!"

Another time, in May 1876, Catherine confessed to her Superior, Sister Dufès, who, marveled by her discourse, suddenly said to her, "You have truly been favored!"

"Oh," replied Catherine, "I am only an instrument. It is not for me that the Blessed Virgin appeared. If she had chosen me, who knows nothing, it was so that we could not doubt her!"

The Life of Catherine Labouré, R. Laurentin,
DDB, 1991, p. 112, 119.

EVERYTHING IS A BLESSING!

On the day of the feast of the Nativity of Mary, September 8, 1876, Sister Catherine fell and hurt her wrist. Seeing her bandage, Sister Dufès asked her, "What happened to you, Sister Catherine?"

"Ah, Sister, I am holding my bouquet of flowers! Every year the Blessed Virgin sends me one like this!"

"The Blessed Virgin takes good care of you!" remarked Sister Dufès.

"When she sends suffering," replied Sister Catherine, "it is really a blessing that she sends to us!"

The Life of Catherine Labouré, p. 130.

LAST RECOMMENDATIONS

In December 1876, Sister Cosnard went to visit Sister Catherine since she was bedridden, due to her declining health. Bending down towards her friend, she asked, "Sister Catherine, are you going to leave me without a single word about the Blessed Virgin?"

Advised Sister Catherine, "You had better pray! May God inspire the Superiors to honor the Immaculate Mary: those are the riches of the community. If we say the rosary well, vocations will be plentiful.... They will lessen if we are not faithful to the Rule, to the Immaculate Conception, to the rosary. We have not served the poor enough! The postulants must go into the hospitals to learn to better themselves.... We must keep them in a state of humility. They must listen to the elders. They must study and learn the doctrine of Vincent (de Paul)."

A little later, Sister Dufès asked her the crucial question, "Sister Catherine, do you not fear death?"

Promptly Sister Catherine responded, "Why should I be afraid to go see our Lord, his Mother, and Saint Vincent?"

The Life of Catherine Labouré, p. 136.

Saint John Neumann, C.Ss.R.

Bishop

Born in the village of Prachatitz in Bohemia (now Czechoslovakia) (1811–1860), the son of a weaver, he was a studious child who thought often of becoming a scientist. When he was twenty, he decided to become a priest. Driven by the need for priests in America, he traveled there. After his ordination, he felt the need for company and spiritual advice and decided to join a religious order. He had met a Redemptorist, was impressed by what he had learned about the order, and decided to join them in Pittsburgh, where they were making their first permanent foundation in America. He was received as a novice and made his vows in 1842. He became the Bishop of Philadelphia in 1852, building some eighty churches, one hundred schools, instituting the Forty Hours Devotion, and helping to map out a plan of Catholic education for the entire United States. He died, as the result of a stroke, in 1860. Pope John XXIII beatified him in 1963 and he was canonized by Pope Paul VI in 1977.

Determination

At the age of twenty, John had to make a career choice between theology, law, or medicine. He felt a great attraction to theology but was wary as only twenty applicants would be accepted out of eighty or ninety. His father, although generally supportive, was not too fond of his choice. His mother, on the other hand, urged him onward. This is his account, explaining his choice:

"Even though I pointed out to her that I did not know anyone who would back my application, she thought I should give it a try. I wrote a letter and sent it to Budweis by a special messenger.... Shortly after that, I received the acceptance.

"From that moment on, I never gave another thought to medicine and gave up completely the study of physics and astronomy, on which I had preferred to spend my time, and this without any great difficulty."

Saint John Neumann: Philadelphia's Little Bishop, Robert H. Wilson,
Archdiocese of Philadelphia: Philadelphia, PA, 1977, p. 5.

GO WHERE YOU ARE NEEDED

After his decision to become a priest, he saw that there was a need for priests for the European immigrants in America, especially those who could speak no English. He packed a small bag and made his way, largely on foot, to the port of Le Havre, where he boarded a boat and spent some forty days at sea, arriving in Manhattan. He was ordained there, in 1836, by Bishop Jean Dubois.

That night, in his journal, he wrote of his resolution for the days and years to come: "I will pray to you that you may give me holiness, and to all the living and dead, pardon, that some day we may all be together with you, our dearest God."

Saint John Neumann: Philadelphia's Little Bishop, p. 9.

A MAN OF MANY TALENTS

A simple man, concerned only with working with his parishioners, he was shaken by his nomination to become a bishop. He appealed to Archbishop Kenrick to ask Rome to reconsider this decision. The Pope, struck by the needs of this diocese (mainly comprised of immigrants) for a multi-lingual leader, remained steadfast. By this time, Father Neumann could speak twelve languages fluently, a fact which greatly influenced Rome.

ACCEPTANCE AND A PRAYERFUL REACTION

The following is an account of Father Neumann's reaction to his impending consecration as Bishop of Philadelphia on March 28, 1852, the day of his forty-first birthday:

Archbishop Kenrick walked down to Saint Alphonsus Rectory and went to Father Neumann's room, as he was wont when going to confession. Finding his confessor out, he laid the episcopal ring and pectoral cross he had himself carried for twenty-one years as Bishop of Philadelphia on the rector's table.

When the rector returned, the sparkle of the ring caught his eye; he asked the Brother porter who had been there. Informed that it was the Archbishop, the full significance of the ring and cross broke into the soul of the priest, who had never wanted any position of authority. He was like a stricken man. He went down on his knees in prayer. Still there and still praying, his brother Redemptorists found him the next morning.

Saint John Neumann: Philadelphia's Little Bishop, p. 16.

ALWAYS READY FOR DEATH

Since New Year's Day of 1860, the Bishop had been feeling weak and dizzy, but told no one. A few days later, he went to dinner and had difficulty recognizing an old friend. When asked, he admitted that he felt a little odd, but that a walk in the fresh air would do him good. Then, he added a rather strange remark: "A man must always be ready, for death comes when and where God wills it."

Bishop John Neumann collapsed in the street that afternoon, suffering a stroke. Loving hands carried him to a nearby house, but he died before the arrival of the priest.

Bishop John Neumann, C.Ss.R.: A Biography, Michael J. Curley,
Redemptorist Fathers: Philadelphia, PA, 1952, p. 394.

SAINT JOHN (DON) BOSCO
PRIEST AND FOUNDER

John Bosco was born in the rural area of Piedmont (1815–1888). After his ordination in 1841, he devoted himself to the education of poor boys in Turin. Helped by a group of volunteers, he founded the Salesians, then the Daughters of Mary Help of Christians. Without a doubt, he was one of the greatest teachers of the nineteenth century.

THOUGHTS OF A FOUNDER

Around 1844, two canons came to Turin to examine the orthodoxy of Don Bosco's projects. One of them asked him, "Well, Don Bosco, are you still considering your work with the youth?"

"If I think about it? Yes, more than ever," exclaimed Don Bosco.

"How do you envision it? Small? Modest?" queried the canons.

"Not at all!" responded Don Bosco, "I see it on a grand scale, enormous, with courses, evening classes, workshops, large classrooms, and a church big enough to hold at least five hundred children."

"And to help you?"

"To help me?" explained Don Bosco. "The priests, catechists, supervisors, teachers, heads of the workshops...."

"What, a whole army!"

"That's the correct word to use," Don Bosco quickly replied.

"But would you be thinking of founding another religious order?" questioned the canons.

"You have said it," he replied.

The canons wanted to know, "What habit will you give to your religious?"

"Well," Don Bosco answered thoughtfully, " I will dress them in virtue!"

Saint John Bosco, A. Auffray, E. Vitte: Lyon, 1937, p. 101.

CONFIDENCE IN THE GENEROSITY OF THE FRENCH PEOPLE

In 1880, Pope Leo XII asked Don Bosco to take over the supervision of the construction of the future Roman Church, to be dedicated to the Sacred Heart. In 1881, Bosco told the Pope: "The venture is beginning to weigh heavy on my old shoulders!"

Not knowing where to find the money, Don Bosco then had the idea of soliciting the charity of the French people. He opened up to a Salesian confrere, Father Bellamy, who answered, "You come at a very bad time, Don Bosco. We are collecting for the Basilica in Monmartre, the foundations of which will gobble up millions. We are also collecting for the Catholic schools that the ill-fated law is forcing us to start. Do you think that the French wallets will open again for this Roman Church?"

"Oh, how little you know about your own country!" countered Don Bosco. "France has money for all needs. She gives unceasingly and tirelessly. In spite of the storms and trials, she remains, for those who know her well—and I am one of them—the generous France!"

Saint John Bosco, p. 250–251.

PROPHETIC ANNOUNCEMENT TO A SICK PERSON

In 1868, Don Rua, Don Bosco's secretary, was just thirty-one years old. Suddenly afflicted by a violent peritonitis, the young priest was soon near death. Recognizing Don Bosco at his bedside, he said to him, in a whisper, "Don Bosco, if my last hour has arrived, don't be afraid to tell me, I am ready for anything!"

"Dear Don Rua," replied the saint, "Do you hear me, I don't want you to die! You still have too much to do."

And Don Bosco blessed him. Returning the next morning, he discovered holy oils on the table of the sick priest. Turning towards the doctor, the priest exclaimed, "What is this here?"

"It is the holy oil for Extreme Unction," replied the attendant Don Savio.

"Extreme Unction for whom?"

"For Don Rua!"

"Who is the brave person who thought of that?" demanded Don Bosco.

"It is I, Don Bosco," confessed Father Savio, who was there. "If you had seen Don Rua last night: it was pitiful! Even the doctor, himself...."

"Ah, people of little faith!" interjected the servant of God. "Listen to me, Don Rua, listen well: even if we threw you out of the window in your condition, you would not die!" In true fact, Don Rua lived for another forty-two years.

Saint John Bosco, p. 258–259.

FAITH TO RAISE THE DEAD

In 1849, Charles N., a young man who had spent fifteen years with Don Bosco died. In his last moments, he had asked to see the priest, but he was away on a trip. When Don Bosco could finally go to see his family in Turin, they said to him, "You are too late! Charles has already been dead for six hours."

"Go away with you," replied Don Bosco, "he is only sleeping!"

The man of God approached the body where his mother and aunt were standing vigil. He blessed it and gathered his thoughts for a long time. Then, he said, with a commanding tone, "Charles, Charles, get up!"

The adolescent's body shuddered. With an abrupt gesture, the priest tore away the shroud which covered his face. Then, getting himself up, the child opened his eyes and began to speak, "Aren't I a mess! Oh, you are here, Don Bosco! If you only knew how I have been calling you! It is God who has sent you. You did well to awaken me."

"Speak, my little Charles, say what you want to say: I am here only for you," comforted the saint.

Answered Charles, "At this time, I truly believe that I should be in the place of eternal sorrow. At one of my last confessions, I hid certain things from the priest. A nasty friend encouraged me to do it. A moment ago, I felt I was being chased by a troop of demons who wanted to capture me, but a beautiful lady interceded by saying: 'Leave him alone: he hasn't been judged yet!' A little later, I heard your voice and woke up. Now, I beg you, hear my confession!"

Petrified in terror, the mother and aunt quickly left the room. When they re-entered with the rest of the family, the confession had been heard. The young man said to the priest, "Don Bosco, you have saved me from hell!"

"Now that you are here by the grace of God, you are assured of your salvation. Do you wish to stay here with us or leave?" asked Don Bosco.

"I want to go to heaven!" exclaimed Charles.

"Well, then, good-bye, Charles, go off to paradise!"

As if he had not anticipated this chance, the child lowered his head onto the pillow, closed his eyes, and resumed his immobility. This time, he went to his eternal rest with the Lord.

Saint John Bosco, pp. 294–296.

A LITTLE POLITICS

On February 7, 1877, Don Bosco was asked to celebrate Mass in the private chapel of François II, the exiled King of Naples. At the lunch which followed, François II suddenly asked Don Bosco, "Well, Father, we who have lost not one, but two kingdoms, can we conquer them again?"

"Sir," replied Don Bosco, "let us think about conquering the kingdom of God, everything is there!"

Replied the ex-King, "Certainly, but what about an earthly kingdom? If you only know how much my faithful subjects miss me and call me back!"

"That is why, sir," said the saint, "God has disposed of it in another way. You can apply the words of Jeremy to this situation: 'Our ancestors sinned; they are no more, and we bear their iniquities' (Lam 5:7). Remember that the Church in Naples had to suffer at the hand of your elders. Such mistakes pass from father to son and one day, the innocent pay for the guilty."

"However, the queen and I have done good things," murmured the King.

"Sir, the good works you do help you even more to withstand the weight of your exile patiently," Don Bosco pointed out.

With some surprise, the King remarked, "Then, your conclusion is that...."

"That your Majesty will never see Naples again!"

"I have dreamed of another future, but I accept this one, if only it could mend the evil my family has done to the Church!" confessed François.

The King asked Don Bosco for his blessing and saw him to the door himself. Later, when the Piedmontese troops arrived in Rome, the royal couple fled to take refuge in Paris. François II died there in 1894, never having seen Naples again.

Saint John Bosco, p. 327–328.

The Count of Cavour, the great architect of Italian unity, was president of the Council and the Minister of External and Internal Affairs in 1860. Having requested that Don Bosco come and explain himself to the ministry, Cavour tried to push the servant of God into a corner. "It is true," the Count noted, "that we have no tangible proof against you, dear Don Bosco, but it is the reigning spirit in your house at Turin which is incompatible with our policies. Regardless of what you say and do, you are with the Pope, hence against us!"

Affirmed Don Bosco, "That is very true, Count, I am with the Pope and I will remain there until my death. But this doesn't stop me from being a good citizen.... Could you cite a single phrase, word, or act of mine that wavers away from the respect due to the authorities? It seems to me that by gathering hundreds of children and keeping them solidly on the road to learning, I honestly contributed to public order. That is my only politics!"

Saint John Bosco, pp. 330–331.

THE BASIS OF ALL LEARNING

Returning from a short stay in Rome in 1858, Don Bosco had a discussion with Cardinal Tosti one morning. He asked him, "In your opinion, Don Bosco, what is the best way to bring up young people?"

Answered Don Bosco, "You see, your Eminence, it seems to me to be impossible to raise them well if you don't win their confidence and love."

"Yes, but how?"

Don Bosco explained, "By doing all we can to bring ourselves closer to them, by breaking down the barriers which keep a distance between us, by working to try to understand and appreciate their likes and dislikes. In short, by trying our best to make ourselves just a little more like them."

Saint John Bosco, p. 339.

DO WHAT IS ESSENTIAL BEFORE WHAT IS URGENT

One day, in the Spring of 1858, two notable Romans came to the Salesian Oratory in Turin to see Don Bosco, who was involved with the children's confessions. He asked Father Cagliéro to tell them, "Ask these gentlemen to wait a while. I can't be disturbed; I am hearing confessions!"

A half-hour passed, then an hour, then an hour-and-a-half: Don Bosco continued to hear confessions. Finally, after an hour and forty minutes, the last penitent left. Now, Don Bosco could go join his illustrious visitors. As an excuse, he simply told them, "Don't be too angry with me, dear friends. You see, you can catch certain birds only in mid-flight; if we miss them, we have no idea when they will return within our reach!"

Saint John Bosco, p. 379.

THE LAST DAY

On the last day of his earthly life, January 29, 1888 (on the feast day of Saint Francis de Sales), Don Bosco said to his secretary, Don Rua, "When I can no longer speak and someone comes to ask for my blessing, you will lift up my hand and make the Sign of the Cross with it, saying the proper words. Me, I will put it in my intentions."

Saint John Bosco, p. 556.

SAINT DOMINIC SAVIO

STUDENT

Dominic was of Italian origin (1842–1857) and a student of Don Bosco. He is actually the youngest canonized non-martyred saint. His favorite saying places this adolescent into the pages of history: "I'd rather die than commit a sin!" He was canonized in 1954.

NEVER ALONE

At about the age of ten, Dominic registered at the Castelnuovo school, approximately four kilometers from his home. He walked this four times a day. A lady, realizing this, asked him, "Little one, aren't you afraid to walk all alone on these roads?"

Dominic replied, "I am not alone; I have my guardian angel with me at all times."

But the lady persisted, saying, "In any event, the trip must be tiresome in this heat, and what's more, you must do it four times a day!"

In answer, Dominic said, "Nothing is tiresome when you work for a boss who pays well."

"And who is your boss?" queried the lady.

"My boss is God, our Creator. He pays the smallest glass of water, given by Him out of love."

Saint Dominic Savio, Don Bosco,
Xavier Mappus: Le Puy, 1965, pp. 40–41.

TEACHER AND STUDENT

Don Bosco welcomed the young Dominic (twelve years old) to his school in Turin: "I think you're good material."

"To what use can you put that material?" asked Dominic.

Don Bosco answered, "To make a habit which we will offer up to our Lord."

Dominic exclaimed, "Then, so I'm the fabric, you be the tailor. Take me with you and make a beautiful habit for our Lord."

"I am afraid that your frail health will not withstand the studies," Don Bosco pointed out.

"Don't worry about that," Dominic responded. "The Lord, who has so far given me health and blessings, will help me again in the future."

"But once you finish studying Latin, what do you want to do?" Dominic's teacher asked.

"If the Lord grants me yet another blessing, I ardently want to become a priest," replied Dominic.

Saint Dominic Savio, pp. 54–55.

THE NICEST GIFT

One day, Don Bosco wanted to offer a gift to encourage his pupil, Dominic, and proposed that he choose it himself. The young man then replied to the priest, "The gift that I ask of you is that you make me a saint. I want to give myself entirely to our Lord, forever!"

Saint Dominic Savio, p. 72–73.

CLOSE TO THE END OF HIS LIFE

On the evening of the March 9, 1857, Don Grassi went to give the last rites to a dying Dominic. As the priest was leaving, Dominic called him back, saying, "Father, before leaving, give me a souvenir."

"Me, but I don't see what I could give you," answered Don Grassi.

Replied Dominic, "Something to comfort me."

Don Grassi replied, "I can think of nothing except to remind you of the passion of our Lord."

"Deo gratis, thanks be to God!" exclaimed Dominic. "May the passion of our Lord Jesus Christ always dwell in my spirit, on my lips, and in my heart!..."

Saint Dominic Savio, p. 170–171.

SAINT THEOPHANES VÉNARD
PRIEST, MARTYR

O riginally from the diocese of Poitiers, Theophanes whose name meant "He who shows God," did just what his name states, in thirty-two years of life on earth (1829–1861). He entered the Foreign Missions Seminary and blossomed there. Ordained in 1852, he left for Vietnam, then became a missionary in Tonkin. Arrested on November 30, 1860, he was decapitated two months later by order of King Tu-Duc.

THE ULTIMATE TESTIMONY

During the time of the persecution of missionaries, a Chinese widow, a fervent Christian, hid Father Theophanes at her home. Betrayed by a member of her family, the young priest was taken away and imprisoned in a bamboo cage. The viceroy had a crucifix brought to him and said to Theophanes, "Crush this cross with your foot and you will not be sent to your death."

Very moved, the priest took the cross into his hands and with great respect, kissed it at length. He then said, "I preached the religion of the cross up until today. How could I renounce it? I don't value this earthly life so much that I would want to keep it to the point of apostasy!"

"If death is so attractive to you, why did you hide? Wasn't it the fear of being caught?" asked the viceroy.

"My religion forbids me from taking my strength for granted and from surrendering myself to you. But since God has decided that I would be arrested, I am confident he will give me the strength to withstand all the forms of torture you may exert and keep me strong until my death."

Just before the execution of his sentence, Theophanes said, "The Lord allowed me to be betrayed by an evil Christian, but I do not begrudge him for it!"

In spite of it all, the judge remarked, "Do not come back and seek revenge on us after your death!"

Replied Theophanes, "No, do not fear this. Far from seeking vengeance, I will pray for you."

Seeing that the Captain of the guard feared that the decapitating sword had lost its edge, Theophanes said to him, "Please, leave it. The longer it lasts, the better it is!"

Effectively, the execution was drawn out and atrocious, but the man of God never lost his state of calm or prayerful meditation.

Two Athletes of Faith, G. Emonnet,
Téquis: Paris, 1988, pp. 217–221.

BLESSED ARNOULD JULES RÈCHE

BROTHER

He was a peasant from the Lorraine region and a mystical carriage driver. He became a Brother of the Christian Schools at the age of twenty-four and Master of the exemplary novices. His earthly life (1838–1890) was woven with marvels in the fabric of his day-to-day life.

LIVE FOR TODAY IN GOD

A Lasalle Brother asked him one day, "Father Director, how can we reduce our sorrows?"

Advised Brother Arnould, "Well, above all, don't think too much about them. Forget those from yesterday: they no longer exist. Don't think of tomorrow's: God will take care of them. Today's sorrows are enough!"

A Lasalle Ascetic, G. Rigault, Ligel: Paris, 1956.

SAINT BERNADETTE SOUBIROUS (OF LOURDES)

CONSECRATED VIRGIN

B orn in Lourdes in 1844, she was the daughter of a poor miller. In 1858, she had eighteen apparitions of the Blessed Virgin Mary. On March 25, the apparition identified herself as being the "Immaculate Conception." In 1866, Bernadette entered the Sisters of Charity of Nevers and lived her life in a quiet and saintly manner until her death on April 16, 1879, an Easter Wednesday. Her final words were "Holy Mary, Mother of God, pray for me, a poor sinner!"

A SOUVENIR FROM THE IMMACULATE CONCEPTION

One day, a person asked Bernadette, who had, by now, become a religious, "Sister, is the Blessed Virgin so beautiful?"

"So beautiful, so very beautiful," replied Bernadette, "that when you see her once, you can't wait to die so you can see her again!"

Bernadette's Logia, R. Laurentin, Médiaspaul: Paris, no. 657.

THE ONLY THING TO FEAR

In 1870, Gougenot des Mousseaux came to the convent at Nevers to question the humble Bernadette, the confidante of the Immaculate Conception. "Sister, the Prussians are at our doorstep. Aren't you frightened?"

"No!" she said with assurance.

"Then, would it be true that there is nothing to fear?" asked Gougenot des Mousseaux.

Replied Bernadette, "I only fear bad Catholics!"

Saint Bernadette Said,
Du Couvent de Saint Gildard: Nevers, 1978, p. 55.

Around the same time, Bernadette wrote to her father, expressing her opinions about current events and she elaborated on the above statement in this way: "I would gladly do without seeing the Prussians, but I am not afraid of them: God is everywhere, even among the Prussians!"

Saint Bernadette Soubirous,
Msgr. F. Trochu, Vitte: Lyon, 1953, p. 427.

LOURDES IS A STEPPINGSTONE, NOT THE END

In 1873, the Bishop of Nevers was preparing to leave for a short visit to Lourdes. Beforehand, he wanted to meet with Bernadette (her name as a religious was Sister Marie Bernard) and made this suggestion: "Sister, do you not want to join us?"

"Monsignor, I made the sacrifice of Lourdes. I will see the Blessed Virgin in heaven, that will be even more beautiful!"

Saint Bernadette Said, p. 79.

THE HUMBLE SERVANT OF THE SERVANT OF GOD

Arriving as a postulant at the Nevers convent, the future Sister Bernard Dalias wanted to find the "confidante of the Blessed Virgin" in the religious community. Giving up, she said to Mother Berganot, "It's strange! I have been here for three days and I have yet to find Bernadette. I am totally mortified!"

Mother Berganot made a sign to one of the Sisters present

who was wearing the veil of a novice and said, "Bernadette, but there she is!"

"That!" exclaimed the new postulant.

Detecting the disappointment in her young companion's statement, Bernadette came and took her hand and said to her, with a smile, "But yes, young lady, it is only that!"

Saint Bernadette Soubirous, pp. 476–477.

A SIMPLE INSTRUMENT OF THE LORD

One Sunday in 1876, Sister Philippine Molinéry was showing a photograph of the Lourdes grotto to Bernadette, hoping to hear her say a few words about the apparitions. Bernadette did not answer her directly, but asked the Sister, "What do you do with a broom?"

Exclaimed Sister Philippine, "What a question! We use it to sweep."

"And afterwards?" continued Bernadette.

"We put it away, behind the door," said Sister Philippine.

"Well, that is my story," said Bernadette. "The Blessed Virgin used me and then put me away. I am happy about this and stay in my place!"

Saint Bernadette Soubirous, p. 475–476.

Later, in 1878, Sister Victoire made this comment to Bernadette one day: "Sister Marie Bernard, you were lucky to remain at the Mother House in Nevers."

Replied Bernadette, "Oh, what else would they have done with me? I am good for nothing!"

"At least here you can pray for those who don't pray," said Sister Victoire.

"I have only that to do. Prayer is my only weapon. I can only pray and suffer!" said Bernadette.

Saint Bernadette Soubirous, p. 534.

A TIME OF TRIAL

Sister Nathalie Manent confided in Bernadette one day, "Sister Marie Bernard, I live here in anguish because I am convinced that our superiors judge me badly and interpret what I do unfavorably."

"But, my poor Sister," counseled Bernadette, "learn to say to yourself: 'Go away, go away, earthly beings! God is what I have and He is enough!'"

Struck by her words, Sister Nathalie soon regained her inner peace.

Saint Bernadette Soubirous, p. 412.

AT THE TIME OF OUR DEATH

One of the Sisters from the Nevers community asked Sister Marie Bernard, "Aren't you afraid of receiving Extreme Unction?"

"Afraid of what?" replied Bernadette.

"Of dying! I would be so afraid if I saw it coming," answered the Sister.

"Oh, we never know when that moment will come. And when it does come, our Lord will give us the strength!" reassured Bernadette.

Saint Bernadette Said, p. 78.

THE TRUE GREATNESS

One day, at the Nevers convent, a little after the distribution of the various duties, Sister Thais said to Bernadette,

"Sister Véronique is of the same profession as I and yet she is a Superior. I'm not: it isn't fair! At least you, Sister Marie Bernard, are the Superior of the Infirmary."

"Me, a Superior?" said Bernadette in amazement. "All I aspire to be is my own Superior and I can't even manage that!"

Saint Bernadette Said, p. 101.

ABOUT THE PRIESTHOOD

In October 1878, Jean Marie Febvre, then seventeen, was preparing to enter the lower seminary, after a somewhat late calling to the priesthood. Thanks to the Chaplain from Saint Gildard, he was able to meet with Sister Marie Bernard in the convent gardens. She asked him, "Do you want to become a priest?"

"Yes Sister, if God calls me," answered Jean Marie.

"Well then,"assured Bernadette,"you will become a priest. Oh, how beautiful it is to see a priest at the altar!" At that moment, the confidante of the Immaculate Conception turned towards the bell tower of the community and added, "But you do know that a priest at the altar is always Jesus Christ on the cross. You will have to work and to suffer, take heart!"

After many hardships at school and with his health, the young man did become a priest. He often told that his fortuitous meeting with Bernadette gave him a special blessing of reassurance which lasted his entire life.

Saint Bernadette Soubirous, pp. 536–537.

ACTIONS AFTER DEATH

A few months before her death, Bernadette was visited in the infirmary by Sister Stanislas, who made this request: "Sister Marie Bernard, I want you to include me in your prayers."

"Yes, yes," promised Bernadette, "I will pray, but not here on earth. I have so little time to live, I am so sick!"

Saint Bernadette Said, p. 106.

Near the end of 1879, each of the Sisters took her turn coming to see Bernadette to confide their various intentions to her so she could present them herself to God, once she passed to the other realm. Bernadette made this promise: "Yes, I will forget no one!"

Saint Bernadette Said, p. 110.

WHY BE SO ATTACHED TO THIS LIFE?

On the eve of her death, Father Febvre asked her before giving her the blessing, "My child, would you now renew the sacrifice of your life?"

Replied Bernadette, "What sacrifice? It is not a sacrifice to leave a poor life in which one has to undergo so many difficulties, to belong to God!"

Saint Bernadette Soubirous, p. 548.

THE FINAL MOMENTS ON THE CROSS

On April 16, 1879, at 2:15 P.M., an hour before taking her last breath, Bernadette was visited at her bedside by Mother Éléonore Cassagnes who said, "Sister, are you suffering very much?"

"All of that is good for heaven," replied Bernadette.

Assured her visitor, "I will ask our Immaculate Mother to console you."

"No, not consolation, but strength and patience!" requested Bernadette.

Saint Bernadette Said, p. 116.

The dying Bernadette stared at the statue of the Blessed Virgin, which was in front of her on the chimney. A moment later, she whispered, "I saw her, I saw her! Oh, how beautiful she was and how anxious I am to go and see her again!"

Saint Bernadette Soubirous, p. 551.

BLESSED MARIAM BAOUARDY
CONSECRATED VIRGIN

Sister Marie (Mariam) of Jesus Crucified (1846–1878), a Christian Arab of Lebanese origin, became a Carmelite, accepted at Pau, France, in 1867. She left for Mangalore, India, in 1870, then returned to Bethlehem in 1875, where she founded a convent. She was favored with a great number of charisms (bodily manifestations of her great sanctity: levitations, stigmata, visions, and other mystical phenomena). She died, stigmatized, at the age of thirty-three. Pope John Paul II beatified her on November 13, 1993—one of the few stigmatics to be so honored.

LANGUAGE OF THE MYSTICS

Between 1873 and 1875, at the Carmel in Pau, the young Sister Mariam, at times, experienced deep and profound meditations. These prompted certain discussions between herself and her Mother Superior, much like as follows:

"Sister Marie of Jesus Crucified, who are you now with?" asked the Superior.

"With the Beloved," answered Mariam.

"What fever do you have now?"

Replied Mariam, "The fever of the languor of love."

"Sister, what do you have?" queried Mariam's Superior.

"I have Love," assured Mariam.

"Then, where are you?" the Superior insisted on knowing.

"In Love," answered Mariam.

Mariam, the Little Arab, A. Brunot, Salvator: Mulhouse, 1981, p. 39.

THE GREAT WAR OF 1914-1918

Sister Mariam had visions about the future and sometimes shared these with her companions. One day in May 1873, her Superior heard her say, "In a few years, a war will happen where there will be rivers of blood shed. It will be a long and cruel war!"

Her Superior asked, "But why such a trial?"

And Mariam replied, "We are corrupt!"

Mariam, the Little Arab, p. 60.

On another occasion, in August 1874, Mariam's Superior asked, "What will happen to the Church at that time?"

Miriam answered, "I believe that all of the priests will be called to fight. Victory will come in due time because France has done too much good in her missions for God to abandon her."

A Summary of the Life of Sister Marie of Jesus Crucified,
D. Buzy, Saint Paul: Paris, 1925, pp. 43–44.

SATAN'S ATTACKS

Sister Mariam was often subjected to demonic attacks. She was not concerned with them and simply repeated this motto: "Go all the way to the finish!" One day when she was stepping up her efforts by washing the clothes for the community, the devil called to her, "God does not expect you to do that much!"

"I work for Jesus: not for you!" replied Mariam.

"If you continue working like that, you will die!" threatened Satan.

"Well," answered Mariam, "then just watch this!" and the Sister scrubbed even harder.

A Summary of the Life of Sister Marie of Jesus Crucified, p. 29.

TO BE WARY OF THE EXTRAORDINARY

In 1874, a foreign prelate came to Pau. He told Sister Mariam, "Sister, in a certain city in Italy, I have admired marvels in the company of a mystic, a visionary. At times, she receives a mystical host from the hands of an angel. Blood runs from her heart and forms various figures, for instance, a crown of thorns. Can you, if you please, give me your feelings about this?"

After having requested a few days to reflect upon this, Sister Mariam said to him, "I prayed to our Lord and asked him to tell me what to make of this person. He told me that, at the beginning, there was some truth in those extraordinary things, but then the devil got involved in it. Actually, it is all from the devil, even the mystical communion afterwards. I did not see that this soul is guilty of anything, not even very far from God. With respect to you, Monsignor, Jesus gave me the job to tell you: do not pay attention to the extraordinary! If someone tells you that the Blessed Virgin appeared somewhere, don't go there, don't bother. Remain firmly grounded in your faith, in the Church, in the Gospels. If, nevertheless, in spite of this warning, you do go to consult the extraordinary, then your faith will weaken. I tell you this on behalf of the Lord!"

The Life of Sister Marie of Jesus Crucified, D. Buzy,
Saint Paul: Paris, 1921, p. 147.

One day, people were speaking in front of Sister Mariam about a person who enjoyed celestial visions and who was spreading enlightening messages. Turning to Mother Élie, the young Carmelite said, "Mother, how I pity these souls! There is so little which is not an illusion. May God protect us from all of this!"

"Then you would not like to be like this yourself?" asked Mother Élie.

Replied Mariam, "I'd sooner die! Mother, one must truly want what God wants. (...) And it is so easy to fall into the sin of pride!"

"Do you know such people?"

"Yes Mother," said Mariam. "I saw a similar one in Alexandria. People came from everywhere for her advice and to ask for her prayers. Her confessor looked upon her as a saint. The first time I saw her, it seemed as if a voice inside of me said: 'It's demoniacal!' I shared my impressions with her confessor, who was also my own. He told me that I was vain. 'You are right, Father,' I told him, 'But if you truly want to find the pathway of that soul, humiliate it, make as if you despise it, many times, because the devil can help withstand a humiliation in order to better mislead the witnesses afterwards.' The priest followed my advice. This soul seemed to withstand the trial, but a little later, she complained that she was misunderstood. She became discouraged. Her extraordinary states stopped, then she abandoned the religious life which she had embraced for a long time."

> *The Life of Sister Marie of Jesus Crucified, Father Pierre Estrate,*
> *Gabalda: Paris, 2nd Ed., 1916, pp. 174–175.*

IN PRAISE OF HONESTY

On December 17, 1875, the porter of a provisional religious house established in Bethlehem died. Two days later, Sister Mariam was mysteriously notified that this saintly man was already in heaven. She confided this to a few religious, who were with her in the Holy Land, "This man was a righteous man. He suffered a great deal, we scorned him, but now, what happiness there is in heaven! Rich persons are honored and are happy on earth for but a few years, but after, they go to purgatory for a long time.... A righteous man is loved by God and, even if he makes a few mistakes, he enlightens him to repent. The devious man, God doesn't even look at him, even if this man has the appearance of being saintly. He is not as pleasing to God as the righteous man, even with all of his imperfections."

The Life of Sister Marie of Jesus Crucified,
Father P. Estrate, pp. 296–297.

GOD IS BEYOND EXPRESSION, REVEALING HIMSELF ONLY TO THE HUMBLE

One day, a Sister asked Mariam, "How do you see the Spirit of God when He comes toward you?"

Answered Mariam, "Angels could not give him a human form and me, a little nothing of dust, how could I give him one? We can never see the Spirit of God as he really is."

"Why?" queried the Sister. "Do we have something covering our eyes?"

"Yes," said Mariam, "the veil of pride!"

The Life of Sister Marie of Jesus Crucified,
Father P. Estrate, p. 401.

THE HIDDEN MARTYR IN DEDICATED SOULS

One day when Sister Mariam was in ecstacy (a mystical state or trance), she exclaimed, "Blessed are those who have given their blood for God!"

"Even happier again," Christ answered her, "are those who make the continuous sacrifice of their lives for my love!"

The Life of Sister Marie of Jesus Crucified,
Father P. Estrate, p. 401.

SAINT FRANCES XAVIER CABRINI

FOUNDRESS

Francesca (Frances) Cabrini was born in Saint Angelo, Italy (1850–1917), the youngest of thirteen children. She grew in laughter and in the love of music. Due to her Mother's and older sister's devotion to the Sacred Heart, Frances followed at a young age, making it the guiding star of her life. Greatly affected by the sanctity of her confirmation, she decided to sacrifice herself to the will of God, in even the smallest things. She told everyone that her dolls were missionary religious, ordering her Mother to remove them as if they were away doing God's work!

The Bishop was so touched by her devotion to, and knowledge about Jesus, that he allowed her to make her first Communion three years ahead of her contemporaries. At the age of eleven, she professed a vow of eternal virginity, renewing it yearly. She began to minister to the poor and the ill, even in those contagious cases where no one else would see to them.

She wanted to join the Sisters of the Sacred Heart as a novice, but was refused because of her age, small stature, and apparent frail health. She met a great amount of hostility in her duties to the sick and poor, even from the Bishop, but this didn't stop her. Finally the Bishop of Todi told her that she could become a missionary Sister, but knowing of no such order, told her to go out and found one.

In 1878, while on a retreat, she vowed to follow a plan of action, not just words. When asked by the Bishop about how her project was coming, she replied that she was looking for a house. In 1880, she found one in Codogno, giving her new order the name, the Missionary Sisters of the Sacred Heart, a name not without controversy, taking nine full years for approval from Rome.

About that time, Bishop Scalabrini of Piacenza told her of Pope Leo XIII's thoughts about the need for missionaries in the United States. He explained that the immigrants to New York were in great need of spiritual guidance. As she had had problems with her foundation in Italy, she saw this as a chance to gain approval for her order and live out her missionary convictions. Receiving the Pope's approval, she left with six Sisters for New York in 1889.

While in the United States, she started sixty-seven orphanages, schools, and hospitals in the span of thirty-five years. She became a United States citizen in 1909 and was canonized in 1946, the first U.S. citizen to become a saint.

A MISSIONARY OF THE SACRED HEART AT THE AGE OF SIX

At the age of six, Frances was convinced of her calling, telling that she would become a missionary and open schools and teach. To her older sister Rosa, she spoke of the Sacred Heart, asking, "Why are the Sisters at the school devoted to the Sacred Heart? Why is Jesus called the Sacred Heart?"

Rosa patiently explained of the mystery of the Holy Trinity and how Jesus, the second person, loved mankind with his human heart.

Frances thought a moment and asked, "In this way, we love the divine heart and his human one, the heart of God and of mankind, all at the same time?"

"Yes, little one," replied her sister.

Asked Frances, "Does everyone in the whole world love the divine heart?"

"No, it is so sad," replied her sister. "Jesus' heart was so good, so lovable, and so loving that he gave his life for all mankind, but he isn't always loved in return. Do you know that there are even people on earth who don't know him? And there are also those who know him, but neglect him!"

Persisted Frances, "How can we show him that we love him? How can we love him for those you spoke about, those who neglect him?"

Her sister answered, "By consecrating ourselves to him, by giving him all that we are and all that we have. He calls us to serve him."

Saint Frances Cabrini, "Without staff or scrip,"
L. P. Borden, Marianopoli: Italy, 1948, pp. 27–28.

JESUS WILL LOOK AFTER ME

One day, when the family was gathering for dinner, a violent earthquake shook their region. Frances could be found nowhere. The family went from room to room in search of her. All of the local citizens were enlisted to look for her. Finally, Rosa found her in the woodshed, where she often went alone to pray. She was on her knees, deep in prayer, eyes lifted to heaven, her face all aglow. Rosa asked, "Little one, something bad has just happened, didn't you notice?"

"Yes, I did," answered Frances.

"It was an earthquake," her sister pointed out worriedly. "Aren't you afraid?"

"No," replied Frances. "Jesus will take care of me."

Saint Frances Cabrini, "Without staff or scrip," p. 43.

A VISIT TO WALL STREET

Once in New York, Mother Cabrini realized that her needs were great, almost as great as those of the people who needed her. So much ambition, yet so few means!

It was her habit to walk along Wall Street, stopping at whatever business office she liked, uninvited, seemingly without a specific purpose.

One day, on such an outing, she stopped and knocked at the door of a local successful businessman, asking to see the President of the company. As she had no appointment, his secretary said:

"Mr. President, Mother Cabrini is here, will you see her?"

He replied, rather gruffly, "What else can I do? She's already here! Give me five minutes only. The quicker I see her, the quicker she'll leave!"

The secretary let Mother Cabrini in to see the President, who greeted her, saying, "Good day, Mother Cabrini, have a seat. I am only seeing you because my secretary insisted. I am so very busy...I only have a few minutes."

Mother Cabrini replied, with a smile, "Oh, I fully understand. Losing time or making someone lose time disgusts me as well. I have come only to ask...."

"For money?" the businessman finished her sentence for her.

"No, not for money!" said Mother Cabrini. "For your advice. I know that you are wise and knowledgeable. I hold your friendship, trust, and faith in me dearly. I value your advice more than money!"

Explaining that she needed his advice to help her find the necessary capital to build a "small" place for one hundred or so orphans, the company President remembered a building he owned which was not being used. Waiting to hear if her plans were realistic, he let her continue. The secretary, in the meantime, entered and informed him that Mother Cabrini's five minutes were up. He told her to go away.

Mother Cabrini continued, "I know of a nice place on the banks of your lovely Hudson River where the children could play and have fresh air. The price isn't too high."

Naturally, this great company President succumbed to the temptation of doing a good deed, how could he resist? He gave her the building in question!

Saint Frances Cabrini, "Without staff or scrip," pp. 137–139.

TO DIE FROM LOVE

Close to her death, Mother Cabrini wrote, "I want to die from love following a life of total self-abandon to God! Jesus, I love you so very much!"

Saint Frances Cabrini, "Without staff or scrip," p. 378.

SAINT THÉRÈSE OF LISIEUX
(OF THE CHILD JESUS)
CONSECRATED VIRGIN

C onsidered by Pope Pius X as "the greatest saint in modern time" (1873–1897), this humble, withdrawn
Carmelite became, in 1925, the principle patron saint
of Catholic missions and, in 1944, the secondary patron of
France, equal to Saint Joan of Arc. She preached and lived
the "little way" of spiritual childhood.

THE PRIORITY OF LOVE

One day in July 1897, at the Carmelite house in Lisieux,
the young Sister Geneviève heard the ringing of the bell
which signaled a change in activities. As she wasn't quick to
leave, Thérèse said to her, "Go to your little duty!"

Then she corrected herself, "No, to your little love!"

Last Conversations, I Enter the Life,
Cerf & DDB: Paris, 1973, p. 227.

In the same month of July, Sister Mary of the Sacred Heart
observed to Thérèse, "How happy we are to die when we
have spent our life in the love of the Lord!"

Responded Thérèse, "Yes, but we must not forget charity
to our neighbor!"

Last Conversations, p. 214.

During her nightly rounds in the infirmary, on August
25, 1897, Sister Geneviève surprised Sister Thérèse, who had

her hands clasped together in prayer. She said to her, "What are you doing? You must try to sleep."

Thérèse replied, "I can't. I am in too much pain, so I pray."

Sister Geneviève asked, "And what do you say to Jesus?"

"I say nothing to him," answered Thérèse. "I simply love him!"

Last Conversations, p. 205.

LIVE THE TRIAL IN LOVE

When, on August 29, 1897, Thérèse was suffering the pain of a martyr in the infirmary, Mother Agnes said, "It is so hard to suffer without any inner consolation!"

Thérèse quickly replied, "Yes, but it is a type of suffering without worries. I am happy to suffer, because that is what God wants!"

Last Conversations, p. 154.

Another time, on August 31, 1897, Mother Agnes asked Thérèse, "If you would die tomorrow, wouldn't you be even a little afraid? It would be so soon!"

"Oh, even if it was tonight, I have no fears. I would only have joy!" replied Thérèse.

Last Conversations, p. 155.

HER MISSIONARY SENSE

One day in May 1897, Sister Mary of the Sacred Heart noticed that Thérèse, already gravely ill, was forcing herself to walk in the lane. Seeing such a clear cut case of foolish disregard, she stated, "Sister Thérèse, you would do yourself more good to rest! This walk (in the garden at Carmel) could do you no good. And it weakens you even more!"

"This is true," answered Thérèse, "but do you know who gives me the strength? Well, I am walking for a missionary... to reduce his fatigue, I offer mine up to God!"

Last Conversations, p. 228.

THE PROMISE AS A FORM OF RETURN

Mother Agnes to Sister Thérèse of the Child Jesus, on July 13, 1897: "You will see us from above, in heaven, right?"

Replied Thérèse, "No, I will come down!"

Last Conversations, p. 73.

On July 17, she came back to this thought, or rather, to the conviction that the Spirit inspires her: "If God grants my wishes, my heaven will be spent on Earth until the end of all time. Yes, I want to spend my heaven doing good on Earth! It isn't impossible, given that even in the beatific vision, the angels watch over us."

Last Conversations, p. 85.

TO KNOW HOW TO GIVE FREELY

On June 11, 1897, Sister Thérèse was throwing flowers towards the statue of Saint Joseph, at the end of the chestnut path. In a childlike and mischievous tone of voice, she said to it, "There, take them!"

Mother Agnes approached and said to the little ailing Sister, "Why are you throwing flowers at Saint Joseph? What blessing are you hoping for?"

Thérèse answered, "Ah, no. It is to make him happy. I do not give in the hope of receiving."

Last Conversations, p. 47.

BODY AND SOUL

On May 20, 1897, Mother Agnes showed her picture to Thérèse, who said, "This is only the envelope. How I would like to see the letter!"

Last Conversations, p. 31.

HOLY SCRIPTURES, ANOTHER CIBORIUM FROM GOD

On May 15, 1897, Mother Agnes confided to Thérèse that she was having difficulties making certain devotional readings recommended by the saints. Thérèse then replied, "For me, I find nothing of interest in books if it's not in the holy Scriptures. That book is enough for me!"

Last Conversations, p. 29.

AN EXAMPLE OF FRATERNAL LOVE

On the orders of the Mother Superior, it was not permitted for the young Sister Mary of the Trinity to speak to Sister Thérèse. It was feared that Sister Mary would catch tuberculosis from Thérèse. One day in June 1897, Sister Mary saw Sister Thérèse in her wheelchair, alone under the chestnut trees. Thérèse made a sign for her to come closer, but the young novice replied with regret, "Oh no, Sister, I don't have permission!"

Overwhelmed with sadness, Sister Mary retreated into a nearby refuge to cry. All of a sudden, as she lifted her head, she was surprised to find Sister Thérèse sitting next to her on the stump of a tree. She said to her, "I am not forbidden to come to you. Even if I should die from it, I want to console you!"

Then, trembling because of the fever, Thérèse laid the head of the young religious next to her heart and dried her tears.

Last Conversations, pp. 232–233.

ABOUT THE GREAT MEETING

In July 1897, Sister Marie of the Eucharist asked Thérèse, "What will you do when you see God for the first time?"

Replied Thérèse, "Just thinking of it makes me happy. What will I do? I will cry out of joy!"

Reported in a letter from Sister Marie of the Eucharist
to M. Guérin, 12-7-1897.

In the infirmary, on June 9, she wrote to Father Bellière, "I am not dying, I am entering life!"

Letters, Saint Thérèse of the Child Jesus,
Cerf & DDB: Paris, 1977, p. 426.

SAINT PIUS X
POPE

Joseph Sarto (1835–1914) was born near Venice of very poor parents. He became a priest, then a bishop and cardinal. He was elected Pope in 1903 and strove to "Restore all in the name of Christ." He was in favor of frequent Communion, and children taking holy Communion at a young age. He reorganized canon law and rose against the modernist currents. He is actually the last Roman Pope to have been canonized.

THE POPE OF THE EUCHARIST

In the Spring of 1912, a mother was allowed a private audience with the Pope. She presented him with her child, aged four years, to have him blessed. Shortly after, the child approached the Pope, put his hands on his knees and fixed his stare on the Pope with confidence. Pius X then asked him, "How old are you?"

"He is four," quickly replied the mother, "and in two years, I hope he will make his first Communion!"

Scrutinizing the clear eyes of the youngster at length, Pius X asked him, "Who do you receive when you take holy Communion?"

"Jesus Christ!" replied the boy.

"And who is Jesus Christ?" asked the Pope.

"Jesus Christ is God!"

Then, turning to the mother, the Pope said, "Bring him to me tomorrow. I will give him holy Communion myself!"

Pius X, the Saint, H. Mitchell, Latine: Paris, 1950, p. 151.

PAPAL POLICY

One day, someone asked Pope Pius X, "Holy Father, what is your policy?"

Then, without hesitation, the Pope pointed to a crucifix nearby and said, "That is my policy!"

Fioretti on Pius X, Paulines: Paris, 1958, p. 162.

THE POPE HIMSELF IS A SERVANT

One day when Pius X entered the Vatican Basilica while being carried in on his "sedia gestatoria," or papal chair, applause sounded loudly everywhere. At once, the Pope bent down towards a prelate who was close by and said in a voice, as firm as it was loud, "We do not applaud the servant in the house of the Master!"

Pius X, the Saint, pp. 220–221.

IN THE NAME OF THE MANDATE JESUS GAVE TO PETER

Even during the life of Pius X, a number of people were healed through his intercession. The following is an account of one of these confirmed cases. One day, two Florentine religious, who were both stricken with incurable ailments, arrived for a private audience with Pope Pius X. They could barely stand up and once they were introduced, said, "Holy Father, would you bless us while asking God to cure us?"

"But why do you want to be cured?" asked the Pope.

"To work for the glory of God!" was their reply.

Pius X placed his hand on their foreheads, blessed them, and added, "Be confident! You will be cured and will work, as you wish, for the greater glory of our Lord."

At that very instant, they were returned to good health.

When someone asked the Pope to explain about his gift of healing, he often replied by referring to the mandate Jesus gave to Peter (Mt 16:19), saying, "I have nothing to do with it: that is the power of the holy keys!"

Pius X, the Saint, p. 214–215.

BLESSED DANIEL BROTTIER
◀○▶

MISSIONARY PRIEST

He was a missionary, a member of the Congregation of the Holy Spirit, sent to Senegal. He was a promoter of the Cathedral at Dakar and dedicated to African history. He was a military chaplain in the First World War with an unwavering dedication. This modern apostle (1876–1936), was given the mandate in 1923, by the Archbishop of Paris, to undertake the direction of the d'Auteuil Orphan-Apprenticeship project. He gave himself to this project to the point of total exhaustion.

MILITARY CHAPLAIN

During the war of 1914, Father Brottier went from one wounded soldier to another, seemingly ignoring the bullets and explosions around himself, only thinking of the salvation of one and all. One day, at the military infirmary, a soldier asked him, "Father, can God forgive me for so many mistakes?"

Replied Father Brottier, "My son, when we speak about sin, the intent is all that matters. Mistakes made without the voluntary intent of displeasing God and hurting mankind are quickly forgiven."

Another soldier then remarked, "Certainly, but how do we make amends?"

"By practicing charity!" he said. "That is what brings us the closest to God."

This Father Had Two Souls, C. Garnier,
The Orphan-Apprentices of d'Auteuil: Paris, 1985, p. 111.

A BEAUTIFUL HEAVENLY FRIENDSHIP

Recently named to head the Orphan-Apprenticeship project, Father Brottier sought an appointment for a meeting with the Archbishop of Paris, Cardinal Dubois. It was November 30, 1923. He wanted to ask him for a favor, "Your Eminence, the d'Auteuil project needs a larger chapel."

Asked the Cardinal, "Yes, but how can that be done?"

"There is a way," suggested Father Brottier. "Couldn't we dedicate it to the Blessed Thérèse of the Child Jesus? This little saint of tomorrow is much loved and very powerful!"

"Don't you think that the patronage of a younger male saint might be more indicated for the boys?" said the Cardinal.

"I don't think so," answered Father Brottier. "Just the opposite! These children were deprived at such a young age of the love of a mother, they have such a void in their hearts that they will surely be drawn to this young saint…. She will be their 'Little Mother' and she will get along with them."

"Oh, well," responded the Cardinal, "if you think of it that way, I willingly give you my approval."

Father Brottier, Y. Pichon, De Gigord: Paris, 1938, p. 122.

THE COMMUNION OF SAINTS

Around the year 1925, a person commented to Father Brottier, "At times, when heaven appears deaf to our prayers, we ask ourselves if the saints have lost their memory!"

"Just the opposite," responded Father Brottier. "They know our needs better than we know ourselves. Believe me, it is the dead who lead the living! We believe that we are in charge of ourselves: in reality, we are lead by the entire group of intercessors and friends we have in heaven…. Personally, I have always entrusted the success of my affairs to them."

Father Brottier, p. 356 & the unedited testimony of M. Margerin.

ONE CURE AMID MANY OTHERS

In 1932, Father Brottier was walking through the chapel when he noticed a young girl on her knees in front of the relics of Thérèse of Lisieux, sobbing as she recited her rosary. Deeply touched, he approached her and asked, "My child, why are you crying in this manner?"

She replied, "Father, I have a sister who is dying in Boucicaut Hospital. In my distress, I have come here to ask Little Thérèse for help."

Then, Father Brottier looked at her steadily and said, "My child, listen to me well: what would you give to Jesus if he healed your sister?"

"Oh, Father," cried the girl, "whatever he wants! I know that he is calling me to the religious life. I will become a religious."

"Then go back to your sister, she is healed."

Upon entering the Boucicaut Hospital, the young girl found her sister completely out of danger. Some time later, following her heart, she entered the religious life with the community at Picpus.

Father Brottier, pp. 361–362.

THE TRUE PRIORITIES

One day, someone asked Father Brottier, "Aren't you just a little too daring? Don't you take Providence or the charity of others just a little too much for granted?"

He replied, "No, because I only seek the glory of God.

Providing that God will be happy and souls will be saved, what else matters?... It is not for me that I work!"

Father Brottier, p. 380.

THE GREATEST PRUDENCE IS CHARITY

One day, Father Brottier welcomed Cardinal Dubois to his office in d'Auteuil. At some point, the Archbishop said to his host, "My dear Father Brottier, don't you think that you're going at it a little too strong? They tell me that you have invested a lot of money in new construction plans for the project. I have been told of an impressive amount of five million!"

"Your Eminence, to be exact, that figure is below the real one. I fear that we must add one or two million more," he said.

Responded the Cardinal, "That is simply foolish! How will you pull that off?"

"The providence of the orphans is there, your Eminence. And then, we always have Little Thérèse!" Father Brottier said confidently.

"I know, I know," admitted the Cardinal, "but the figures scare me. I truly feel that your generosity has carried you too far. They tell me that you accept the orphans without concern, throwing the doors open to all. Have you even thought about the future?"

Father Brottier replied, "Precisely, I never stop thinking about that, your Eminence, but how could I have the heart to reject and push these poor little ones out the door?"

"In the meantime, you must, Father. Sometimes we must! It is necessary for our sense of reason to have control over the impulses of the heart. It is a thankless thing I tell you, but it is my job to remind you of prudence," said the Cardinal.

At this point in the conversation, there was a knock at the door. As there was a sign hanging there which said "knock and enter," the door opened. A poor woman and a young boy of thirteen entered. Father Brottier questioned her with his customary kindness, "What do you want, Madam?"

"Father, I am a widow, I am poor, I am sick. Soon I will have to go to the hospital. Will I ever be able to leave the hospital? It is not certain. My son has no one else but you!"

Father Brottier remained silent. The poor woman, worried, turned her glance alternately to Father Brottier and then to the older priest who was also seated there, watching her in silence. Finally, Father Brottier said, "Madam, it is not I who will decide your child's destiny. You are fortunate: here, before you, is the Archbishop of Paris. He, himself, will answer you!"

The old Cardinal smiled, then said, "Since the question was asked in this manner, I will resolve this situation right now. It is yes, dear lady! Father Brottier will take your child. Rest assured of your child's future."

The poor widow, much happier, left with her child, not knowing how to show her gratitude. Once she had left, the Cardinal called upon Father Brottier, saying, "Well, my dear Father, congratulations! I reproached you earlier, now, I should do the same to myself! Oh, how you have trapped me!"

"I protest the idea that I trapped you, your Eminence. It wasn't me!"

"Then who?" asked the Cardinal.

"The Lord!" was Father Brottier's reply.

Father Brottier, pp. 167–169.

When Silence Speaks

One day, with a smile, Father Brottier said to a friend and confrere, Father Pichon, "I just met with a woman who spoke to me for a half-hour. Note that apart from the necessary formalities of 'Hello' and 'Good-bye,' I said absolutely nothing: not a single word! All I did was listen to a recitation of her problems. She spoke at great length. She let her sorrows flow freely. She cried and, finally, she was appeased. She left consoled and full of courage. Do you know what she said to me when she left? Literally, this is it: 'Oh Father, how good you are! How you have consoled me with what you have said! How your words have made me feel better!'

"You can see by this how easy it is sometimes to be useful: by being silent, letting people speak, understanding their worries, by sympathizing, showing them friendship and love…. Often, we have to do nothing more than this to put a soul back onto the right track!"

Father Brottier, p. 426.

BLESSED RUPERT MAYER, S.J.
PRIEST

Rupert Mayer (1876–1945) was born in Stuttgart and entered the Jesuits in 1900. He became, from 1912 to 1945, the person they called "The Apostle of Munich." He preferred to walk freely to prison and death rather than be silent about evangelical truth. His tomb in Munich, where they no longer count the cures (as there are so many), draws immense crowds from all parts of the world. He was beatified in 1987.

A FEW REASONS FOR A RELIGIOUS VOCATION

Around the age of sixteen, Rupert declared his intention of becoming a Jesuit priest to his father, who objected, "You let yourself be influenced!"

"No," said Rupert, "and I can give you three reasons why I prefer to enter the Jesuit order: these people are persecuted everywhere; they educate the youth in a remarkable fashion; and finally, they receive training themselves which best prepares them to fight for God."

"Oh well," said his father, "that may be, but you will only enter after you do one year of diocesan ministry. Then, you will be the required age and you can more freely commit yourself."

That was how it was done.

Father Mayer, the Apostle of Munich,
A. Koerbling, Chalet: Paris, 1987, p. 11.

MILITARY CHAPLAIN IN THE GREAT WAR

During the heavy fighting in the Summer of 1915, there was always a man at the front lines, going from one person to another, offering encouragement or gathering the wounded: that was Father Mayer. One day, fighting was so heavy that nurses abandoned the stretcher where a wounded soldier lay, moaning in pain. Suddenly, Father Mayer arrived, laid across him and said, "Lay still, my friend! If anyone is touched, it will be me first!"

Father Mayer, the Apostle of Munich, p. 26.

KINDNESS RATHER THAN HARSHNESS

Father Mayer had been called to the bedside of a dying woman, who said, "Thank you for your visit, but no thanks for the last rites!"

"Allow me to step out for a moment," said Father Mayer.

The priest left the room and came back a few minutes later with a magnificent bouquet of flowers. With a smile, he offered them to the dying woman with the explanation, "It truly worries me to see you leave for eternity in this state. So, I had the need to make you happy one last time!"

Touched by this gesture of pure kindness, the dying woman wanted to make her final confession and died shortly after.

Father Mayer, the Apostle of Munich, p. 45.

AT THE ORIANENBURG CONCENTRATION CAMP

Imprisoned at the Orianenburg concentration camp at the end of December 1939, Father Mayer used the opportunity to pray even more and study. In April 1940, he received the order that he would leave the camp in a half-hour for an unknown destination. He confided to his companions, "Whatever may happen to me from now on, I look to the future with a perfectly calm spirit because I have given the sacrifice of my life!"

Father Mayer, the Apostle of Munich, p. 82.

BLESSED ELIZABETH OF THE TRINITY
◄○►
CONSECRATED VIRGIN

E lizabeth Catez was born near Bourges (1880–1906) and felt called to the Carmelites at an early age. She was able to enter the Dijon community at the age of twenty-one in 1901 and there she led a life that was simple and bathed in prayer. Her avowed goal was to become, herself, a pure praise of glory to the Blessed Trinity. She was beatified in 1985.

ALWAYS GO TO THE ESSENTIAL

From the time of her entry into the Carmelites, Elizabeth had to respond to the following questions, asked in writing by the Novice Mistress: "What is, according to you, the model of holiness?"

Elizabeth: "To live in love."

Novice Mistress: "What is the fastest way to get there?"

Elizabeth: "By making oneself small, to give oneself without expectation of return."

Novice Mistress: "What is your favorite virtue?"

Elizabeth: "Purity: 'Blessed are the pure of heart, for they will see God.'"

Novice Mistress: "What is the fault that displeases you the most?"

Elizabeth: "Egoism, in general."

Novice Mistress: "Could you give a definition for prayer?"

Elizabeth: "The union of the person who is nothing with He who is everything."

Novice Mistress: "What is your favorite book?"

Elizabeth: "The soul of Christ, because it brings me all of the secrets of the Father, who is in heaven."

Novice Mistress: "What name would you like to have in heaven?"

Elizabeth: "The Will of God!"

The Spiritual Doctrine of Sister Elizabeth of the Trinity,
M. Philipon, DDB: Paris, 1954, pp. 31–32.

THE SOUL OF CHRIST

On her first night at Carmel, Elizabeth went to reflect for a time at the foot of the great crucifix which dominates the garden of the cloister. Mother Germain approached her and gently asked, "What are you doing there, my child?"

Elizabeth replied, "I have stopped for a visit into the soul of my Christ!"

The Spiritual Doctrine of Sister Elizabeth of the Trinity, p. 154.

HOW A CONTEMPLATIVE RELIGIOUS SERVES HER COUNTRY

A priest had commented to Elizabeth how the religious people of France were suffering under the anticlerical civil laws. She replied, "Poor France! I would like to cover her with the blood of the Just One."

The Spiritual Doctrine of Sister Elizabeth of the Trinity, p. 245.

LAST ADVICE

A few days before the death of Elizabeth, a Sister, assigned to domestic chores, came to ask Elizabeth to pray for her. She asked her to explain exactly what her mission would be when she arrived in heaven. Not able to speak any longer, she wrote her answer on a piece of paper: "It seems to me

that in heaven, my mission will be to attract souls by helping them go beyond themselves in order to join God through
a simple movement, all loving, and to keep them in the great
inner silence which allows God to imprint Himself in them
and transform them into Him."

The Spiritual Doctrine of Sister Elizabeth of the Trinity, p. 272.

The evening before her death, her last intelligible words
were "I am going to the Light, to Love, to Life!"

The Spiritual Doctrine of Sister Elizabeth of the Trinity, p. 52.

SAINT EDITH STEIN

CONSECRATED VIRGIN

Edith Stein (1891–1942) was born in Breslau into a family of merchant Israeli Jews. As a student, she took courses from Husserl and Max Scheler. She converted and was baptized a Catholic in 1922 and became a professor of German. She wrote many works of philosophy, became a Carmelite in 1934, and received the name Teresa Benedicta of the Cross. She offered her life for the Jewish people, remaining firm in her convictions right to the very end of her life. She was deported by the Nazis for being both Jewish and baptized. She died in Auschwitz in 1942, and was canonized on October 11, 1998. Husserl made this beautiful testimony to her life: "For her, all is absolutely true!"

THE OLD AND NEW ALLIANCE

In 1934, Edith admitted, to her mother, her fervent desire to enter the Carmelites. Her mother then took her to a nice service at the neighborhood synagogue. On their way home, she questioned her daughter, with some anxiety, "Wasn't the Rabbi's sermon beautiful?"

"Yes, of course," replied Edith.

"We can be devout then, and still remain a Jew?" asked her mother.

Replied Edith, "Certainly, if we know nothing else!"

Edith Stein, by a cloistered French religious,
Seuil: Paris, 1954, p. 134.

About Saint Thérèse of the Child Jesus

One day in 1933, Sister Aldegonde admitted to Edith that she didn't appreciate the style of Thérèse of the Child Jesus at all. Edith then quickly scribbled, on a piece of paper, the answer she would have liked to have given to her friend verbally, "Up until then, I have not even considered that we could dare to speak about the little Thérèse in this manner. My only impression is to have found myself there, faced with a human life, uniquely and totally lived to the very end through the love of God. I know of nothing greater. I would like to bring a little of that for my own life and for that of those around me, as much as possible."

Edith Stein, by a cloistered French religious, p. 114.

The Future and Prayer

One day a student friend of Edith's asked her, "Can you advise me about my future?"

"Let us pray together to get an answer from God. We must ask him to let us know what he wants from you," advised Edith.

Edith Stein, by a cloistered French religious, p. 84.

Self-Abandon to Providence

At the beginning of August 1942, Edith was transported to the north of Holland to a military transit camp, in Westerbork. Two Christian emissaries were admitted there for a short humanitarian visit. They were young people, friends of the Carmelite community in Echt. One of them said to Edith, "We don't know how to express our sympathy to you."

"No matter what happens," replied Edith, "I am ready for anything. The Child Jesus is also here with us…. Hence, don't concern yourselves with me: I know that I am in God's hands!"

Edith Stein, by a cloistered French religious, p. 203.

LAST MESSAGE

Edith succeeded in passing a message from Westerbork, to her Sisters in Echt, on the eve of her departure for Auschwitz. In it, we can read her own reflection, which perfectly summarizes her experiences at that time: "We cannot gain a 'knowledge about the cross' unless we begin by truly suffering for the cross. From the first moment, I had an intimate conviction about it and I said from the bottom of my heart: Hail to the cross, my single hope!"

Edith Stein, by a cloistered French religious, p. 204.

Saint Maximilian R. Kolbe

Priest

Maximilian Kolbe (1894–1941) was born in Poland, became a Conventual Franciscan, and, in spite of his poor health, initiated a variety of missionary endeavors in Poland and Japan. He was a fervent apostle who said that he wanted to win all souls for Christ through the Immaculate Conception. He was imprisoned in May 1941, in the Nazi concentration camp at Auschwitz. At the end of July of the same year, he asked to die in the bunker (where prisoners were starved to death) in place of another, the father of a family. He died during the vigil on the eve of the feast of the Assumption. He was canonized in 1982.

Help Yourself, Heaven Will Help You

Around 1926, at the convent in Grodno, Poland, Father Kolbe kept developing the print shop and increasing the numbers of subscribers to his missionary magazines. One day, a bishop came to examine him more closely and expressed a veiled criticism, saying, "Dear Father, what would Saint Francis do if he saw these expensive machines?"

"Well Monsignor, he would roll up his sleeves and get to work with us!"

The Secret of Maximilian Kolbe, M. Winowska,
Saint Paul: Paris, 1971, p. 106.

Real Progress

Just before the war, at the Niepokalanow convent, Father Kolbe was questioned by his young Franciscan brothers, "Tell us, Father, according to you, to what can we attribute the real progress of Niepokalanow?"

"It is surely not due to the enlargement of the property nor the increased number of machines, not even to another increase in our subscriptions. In fact, the real Niepokalanow does not consist of our visible activities, inside the cloister or even outside. No, the real Niepokalanow is our souls! All the rest, even technology, is secondary. The progress is therefore spiritual, or it is not at all!"

The Secret of M. Kolbe, pp. 139–140.

IN AUSCHWITZ

At the end of July 1941, in the Auschwitz concentration camp, great sanctions were put into force because a prisoner had escaped and had not been found. At some point, Father Kolbe found himself standing next to a young boy who was trembling with fear. Gently, he said to him, "You are so afraid, my poor little one? Don't be afraid, death isn't so frightening!"

The Secret of M. Kolbe, p. 172.

THERE IS NO GREATER LOVE THAN TO GIVE ONE'S LIFE

At the end of July 1941, Langerfuhrer Fritsch decided to send ten more men to the starvation bunker in retaliation for the escape of a prisoner from Cell Block 14. He made the selection himself. One of the condemned men cried out, in spite of himself, "My poor wife and children: I will never see them again!" The ten men were all ready to leave when Father Kolbe stepped out of the ranks. Fritsch questioned him harshly, "What does this Polish pig want?"

"I wish to die in the place of one of the condemned men," stated Father Kolbe.

"Why?" demanded Fritsch.

Father Kolbe replied, "I am old and good for nothing. My life is no longer of any use."

"Who do you want to die for?" demanded the camp commander.

"For this one here: he has a wife and children," maintained Kolbe.

Insisted Fritsch, "But who are you?"

"A Catholic priest," answered Father Kolbe.

A moment of silence followed. Finally, Fritsch made his decision: "So be it, go with them!"

Quickly, the exchange between the two prisoners took place. The Franciscan priest left with the nine others, not only to die with them, but also to help them die.

The Secret of M. Kolbe, pp. 176–177.

ANONYMOUS

Among the immense group of chosen souls, there are so many saints who are not canonized! So many who are unknown or misunderstood! In conclusion, for the present collection, exclusively devoted to official sanctity, permit us to mention a more recent case, not yet recognized by Rome. It is a good example of inspired words and that the union between God and the most authentic is not necessarily a matter of canonical and universal acceptance. Rather, it is the daily hidden mystery of any soul in a state of grace, that is to say, it is any lasting form of the total gift of self in the breeze of the Holy Spirit.

AT BEST, ACCOMPLISH THE WILL OF JESUS

In 1971, a young girl of twelve years of age, mentally handicapped as the result of meningitis in early childhood, was accidentally burned on ninety percent of her body. She had recently made her first Communion.

This young girl lived her trial with an angelic patience. Soon, there was an operation to amputate a limb. After the operation in a Paris hospital, a religious went to speak with her. Realizing her exceptional fervor, she suddenly asked her, "What would you prefer, to stay here with us or to go to heaven?"

"Here, I am with Jesus. In heaven, it would be the same. I would prefer to do what He wants!"

A little later, she went into a coma, and, a month later,

she died, or rather made the glorious paschal passage toward the source of all happiness, God.

The Spiritual Life, Paris, October, 1971, p. 144ff.

CONCLUSION

O ur bouquet of flowers is now complete! Certainly, other flowers could have been chosen, but these seemed to have been picked among the most sure, the most beautiful, the most inspired.

Our floral homage, we realize, doesn't evoke peremptory or severe reactions, but comments expressing religious zeal and happiness, which, by their evangelical nourishment, reach deep into the human heart and say something about the God of Jesus Christ.

Could we not ask the same thing of all Christians: entrust me with your spontaneous comments, I will tell you who you are and where you are with the Lord.

No matter what saints expressed themselves in these pages, their answers are never harmful. To the contrary, they breathe joy and are always inspired by a great love for God and for our neighbors. What comforting food for our gray world, which is prey to so much aggression!

From Saint Peter to Father Kolbe, the road is long, often narrow, but always lit by the Holy Spirit who loves to come and live in the midst of the children of mankind. We have retained numerous and saintly words, but the reader could find even more if he/she would go and read more about the lives of the saints. He/she would just have to read the biographies which are best authenticated by history and documents. It is there that the reader would have the best opportunity to find evangelical gems.

May this book put you on the road to a living knowledge of the friends of God, you and all of us alike. May it stimulate us all to join them in their closeness to the Lord!

BROTHER BERNARD-MARIE
BROTHER JEAN HUSCENOT

OTHER WORKS
BY BROTHER BERNARD-MARIE

La Passion selon la Bible (The Passion According to the Bible), Saint Paul: Paris, 1980.

Prier le Rosaire avec la Bible (Pray the Rosary With the Bible), Saint Paul: Paris, 4th ed., 1985.

Mon 1er voyage au pays de Jésus (My First Trip to the Land of Jesus), illustrated by Olivier Nalet, Chalet-Novalis: Paris and Ottawa, 1987.

Le Père Crozier, l'ami stigmatisé du Père de Foucauld (Father Crozier, the Stigmatized Friend of Father de Foucauld), Chalet: Paris, 1988.

Mon 1er voyage au pays de François d'assise (My First Trip to the Land of Saint Francis of Assisi), illustrated by O. Nalet, Chalet: Paris, 1989.

Des lieux pour mieux prier (Places Conducive to Prayer), Chalet: Paris, 1990.

La Foi à trois voix (Faith With Three Voices), Chalet: Paris, 1991.

L'Ange de Tobie: Messe, Prières et Pensées pour tous les jours (The Angel of Tobias: Masses, Prayers and Meditations for Every Day), Chalet: Paris, 6th ed., 1993.

Mon Dieu, je t'aime très fort: premières prières (My God, I Love You: First Prayers), Chalet: Paris, 3rd ed., 1993.

L'Évangile de Marc: Sacy révisé (The Gospel of Mark: Sacy revised), Chalet: Paris, 2nd ed., 1993.

Le Rosaire des humbles (The Rosary of the Humble), Chalet: Paris, 8th ed., 1994.

Prières pour les causes difficiles ou désespérées (Prayers for Difficult and Desperate causes), Chalet: Paris, 10th ed., 1994.
Chemin de Croix et d'amour (The Way of the Cross and Love), Chalet: Paris, 4th ed., 1994.
Le Pardon de Dieu (God's Forgiveness), Chalet: Paris, 2nd ed., 1994.

Please note: to the best of our knowledge, the above books are not currently available in English. The English titles, in parenthesis, are provided for informational purposes only.

OTHER WORKS
BY BROTHER JEAN HUSCENOT

Vers toi, Notre Dame (Toward You, Our Lady), General Book
  Office: Paris, 1974.

L'École? Au poteau! (School? On trial!), Téquis: Paris, 1976.

L'homélie en question (The Homily, Questioned), D. Guéniot:
  Langres, 1980.

Prier avec Saint François d'Assise (Pray with Saint Francis of
  Assisi), J. P. Delarge: Paris, 1981.

Prier avec Saint Ignace de Loyola (Pray with Saint Ignatius of
  Loyola), Ed. J.P. Delarge: Paris, 1981.

Les sources de l'École chrétienne (The Source of the Christian
  School), OEIL: Paris, 1984.

Le Curé d'Ars, ce n'est que ca (The Curé of Ars, It's Only That),
  OEIL: Paris, 1986.

Notre saint de ce jour, douze livrets mensuels (Our Saint of the
  Day: Twelve Monthly Booklets), OEIL: Paris, 1986.

Les saints aux cheveux blancs (The Saints With White Hair),
  Médialogue: Paris, 1988.

La sainteté par l'école (Sanctity Through School), D. Guéniot:
  Langres, 1989.

Saint Louis, roi de France (Saint Louis, King of France), Téquis:
  Paris, 1990.

Ces chrétiens qui ont fait l'Europe (Those Christians Who Built
  Europe), Fleurus: Paris, 1990.

La sainteté avant 30 ans (Sainthood Before the Age of Thirty),
  Chalet: Paris, 1991.

Le signe de croix (The Sign of the Cross), Chalet: Paris, 1992.

Please note: to the best of our knowledge, the above books are not currently available in English. The English titles, in parenthesis, are provided for informational purposes only.

THEMATIC INDEX

TABLE OF SAINTS
IN ALPHABETICAL ORDER

TABLE OF SAINTS
IN CHRONOLOGICAL ORDER
—◦—

ABOUT THE AUTHORS

———◆◇◆———

Bernard-Marie, O.F.S., is a member of the Third-order Franciscans and is a theologian, Bible scholar, and expert in Franciscan spirituality. He is the author of more than a dozen other spiritual books.

Jean Huscenot, F.É.C., is a Brother of the Christian Schools, a teacher, and the author of a number of books on religious history.